FIJI
Celebration

FIJI CELEBRATION BY JAMES SIERS

First published 1985 by Caines Jannif Ltd.,
Victoria Parade, Suva, Fiji

ISBN 0-312-28930-8

JAMES SIERS

FIJI

Celebration

ST. MARTIN'S PRESS
NEW YORK

INTRODUCTION

This is my celebration of Fiji — a selection of plates showing everything that I have found attractive about the islands and the people in more than 20 years of happy association. Its soft south seas climate, its smiling generous, hospitable people, its varied topography, has cast a romantic spell on me as it has on many people who have found their way to its shores. As the young nation develops its resources, much attention is being paid to the promotion of tourism so that others can discover a destination where people are genuinely friendly and where the landscapes and seascapes are as beautiful as the brochures show.

Fiji has been the cross-roads of the Pacific since the dawn of pre-history. It was here that the Polynesian race, as we know it today, evolved from a mixture of Melanesian and Malay-type peoples. Eventually the islands became a Melanesian domain, but with a Polynesian culture which allowed the rise of powerful chiefly families and states. Its vast physical resources attracted people from Tonga, Samoa, Wallis Island, Rotuma and at least once, from far away Kiribati. It is a beautiful landscape, full of the most wonderful variation. There are some 333 islands in the archipelago, varying in size from the large land masses of Viti Levu and Vanua Levu to tiny little coral specs and atolls. There are rugged volcanic peaks, great rivers and forests and an infinitely changing coastline.

This varied landscape is home to more than 646,000 people, of whom 287,952 are indigenous Fijians, representing 44.5% of the population; 323,707 Indians, 50.7% of the total population; 11,145 part-Europeans; 4,408 Europeans; 8.073 Rotumans; 4,603 Chinese and 6,341 other Pacific Islanders. It is a fascinating mix of cultures and faiths. It is not possible to think of Fiji without thinking of its people. The Fijians today are regarded as the friendliest people in the Pacific — possibly the world. This is one of the reasons why the growth of tourism is so spectacular. The friendliness and hospitality are based on traditional values and can sometimes be easily abused by well-meaning visitors. The Indian population, mainly descended from indentured labourers, has its own rules of hospitality and though this may not necessarily be as outgoing as that of the Fijians, it is just as genuine.

More than 200,000 visitors come to enjoy Fiji every year and the number is growing rapidly. Most visitors come to relax and to enjoy the beaches and the resorts, with occasional forays to one of the towns to take advantage of duty-free shopping. The more adventurous find their way into the countryside and to some of the out of the way places. There is in Fiji something for everyone.

This volume tries to show in pictures the attractive aspects of Fiji, both the country and its people. There is an outline of its history as well as a supplement of facts which many curious visitors may want to know. For those who would want to know more, a visit to the Fiji Museum in Suva will prove worthwhile. The Museum has an excellent display and has also issued in facsimile several books published in the last century. Visitors who want to get good advice should seek it at the officers of the Fiji Visitors Bureau in Suva or at the International Airport, Nadi. Many are confused by the difference between written and oral Fijian. This is due to a system of orthography devised by the missionaries William Cross and David Cargill during the last century and which is in use to this day. For those who are not familiar with it, the following should be noted:
B is MB as in *number* — Bau is pronounced Mbau;
C is TH as in *that* — Cakobau is pronounced Thakombau;
D is ND as in *end* — Nadi is pronounced Nandi;
G is NG as in *sing* Toganivalu is pronounced Tonganivalu;
Q is NGG as in *younger* — Beqa is pronounced Mbengga.

There are many people who have discovered Fiji who keep coming back. This is the type of recommendation which always speaks louder than words. It is also said that one picture is worth a thousand words and I would hope the rule would apply to the selection of colour plates and to the wonderful pictures from the archives which show something of Fiji as it was.

But whatever your reaction, it is certain that Fiji will have proved a different experience.

Lagoon, village and island, Lomaiviti.

Nadi Bay is studded with perfect little islands; to the west and north lie the Mamanuca and Yasawa Islands.

This view is of Malolo Lailai and Malolo Islands.

Nadrau village, interior Viti Levu.

Waya Island village, Yasawa Group.

Ba Gap, Western Viti Levu.

Canefields on the way to Natadola.

Natadola beach, one of the finest on Viti Levu.

One of the islands in Bau waters, Lomaiviti.

Road to Yalavou, Viti Levu.

Horseman, Sabeto Valley, Nadi.

Sunset, Nalebaleba, upper Sigatoka River.

Trekking into the interior, upper Sigatoka River, Viti Levu.

Newly-planted Kasava.

Lower Sigatoka River valley.

Patchwork of sugarcane fields, north-west Viti Levu.

Sugarcane harvest near Ba.

Sakiasi Butadroka planting dalo on his property near Suva.

Kings Road landscape near Nausori.

An aerial view of the Fijian Hotel, one of the first luxury resorts built in Fiji.

The Castaway Hotel resort in the Mamanuca Islands enjoys a superb location.

Tobacco fields on the banks of the Sigatoka River.

Wainimala River view, eastern Viti Levu.

Buca Bay, Vanua Levu.

Ra coast as seen from the air.

Scenes from the Coral Coast.

Nalebaleba, Upper Sigatoka River valley.

Cabbages, upper Sigatoka River valley. Sugarcane, tobacco, passionfruit, papaya, potatoes, tomatoes, corn and all kinds of vegetables are grown in the valley.

Cooling down in a pool of your own in the superb Yasawa Islands is one of the reasons they are popular.

A Blue Lagoon cruise boat at Nanuya Lalilai, Yasawa Islands.

A *bure*, interior Viti Levu.

Sorting cured tobacco leaf, Nalebaleba, Upper Sigatoka River valley.

Suva as seen from the air, looking towards Suva Point.

The new guard marching to the gates of Government House, Suva.

Views of Fiji, featuring the office of the Fiji Visitors Bureau, the Burns Philp building, Renwick Road and the band of the Fiji Military Forces on Victoria Parade.

Yachts at the Bay of Islands, Suva; the Garrick Building; Mosquito Island, Bay of Islands; Victoria Parade.

The diversity of Fiji's ethnic mix is reflected in the faces of the people.

A Muslim bride, her face revealed for the camera, sits gravely.

A Hindu wedding is a colourful ritual.

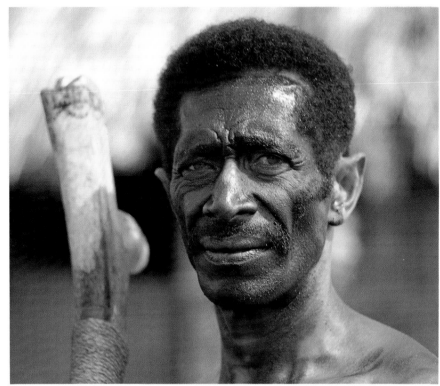

Masi cloth made from the bark of a tree is still used by Fijians for ceremonial occasions.

Parading the Colours, Albert Park, Suva.

Fijian troops won distinction in the war against Japan in the Pacific and during the emergency in Malaya. Since then they have served in various peace-keeping missions in the Middle East.

The Fijian firewalking ritual being demonstrated at Pacific Harbour. The stones are heated over several hours, the unburnt wood and embers are removed, the stones are levelled and then the initia[tes] walk across the pit. The first across the pit is the *bete* (priest) and behind him rises the tall roof of the *bure kalou* (pre-Christian temple).

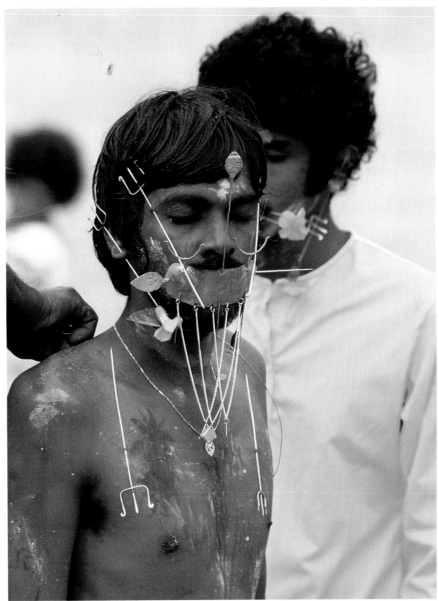

The Indian community also has a firewalking ritual. This is religious demonstration of faith to show that the mind (or spirit) is stronger than the flesh. For those who have faith there is no pain when their bodies are pierced by skewers and no burning when they walk across the pit of embers.

One of the most important Fijian rituals is the presentation of the *tabua*. This is the tooth of the sperm whale which has a power far beyond its intrinsic value. In olden days it was the price of life and death, while today it is indispensible to all formal occasions. The proper mode of presentation is demonstrated at the Orchid Island Cultural Centre.

...ore the introduction of cloth, Fijians relied on cloth made from the bark of a tree and known as *masi*, but now also increasingly known as *tapa*. The way it was worn for festive occasion is shown here against a background of the *bure kalou* at Orchid Island.

The proper preparation and serving of *yaqona* (also known as *kava*), is extremely important on formal occasions. The drink is made from the dried root of the shrub *piper methusticum*. The root is first pounded into a powder and then mixed with water in a special bowl reserved for its exclusive use. The undissolved particles are strained out with hibiscus fibres and the infusion is ready to serve. Each stage of the preparation and serving is accompanied by chanting and clapping and is critically observed by the assembly. This sequence was filmed at Orchid Island.

e is a general description of various Fijian dances and theatrical
entations. These vary from vigorous men's club and spear dances
ulating battles, to graceful women's posture dances. *Mekes* accompany
nal occasions in conjunctions with the rituals of *tabua* presentation and
serving of *yaqona*.

Prince Charles at Levuka in 1970 on the occasion of Fiji's independence. It was also here in 1874 that the Deed of Cession was signed by Ratu Seru Cakobau and other chiefs and commemorated by a plaque set into a stone.

Churches, mosques and temples abound in Fiji reflecting the country's ethnic mix. Shown here are the Muslim mosque at Sigatoka; the Centenary Wesleyan church in Suva; the Catholic cathedral in Suva and the Hindu temple, also in Suva.

Children playing rugby in a stream near Navua.

An Eastern Selection playing the Wallabies at Suva. Fijians love rugby and are the world champions in 7-a-side rugby played in Hong Kong each year.

An echo of Fiji's colonial past is seen in this architecture.

A feature of the Western Division is the yearly Carreras charity horse race at Votua Levu. This includes a series of events, such as bareback riding; relays and a cross-country race where not all get across the river successfully.

Water skiing at the Fijian Hotel, Coral Coast.

A busy scene in the lagoon with a large net laid and line fishermen nearby.

Fish drive at Natadola.

Various forms of fishing in Fiji: from a *bilibili* on the Sigatoka River; using a throwing spear at Taveuni, and underwater spearfishing in Nadi Bay.

Fish vendor's punt in Nabukulau Creek, Suva.

Smoke-cured octopus at the Nadi market.

Suva markets.

An aerial view of Levuka.

Levuka scenes: The Catholic school; Morris Hedstrom store — it was here
that the company began its business empire; Tui Levuka's *bure*; Beach Str

A baby being bathed in the upper Sigatoka River; a young boy about to jump into a clear pool at Taveuni.

Copra plantation and cattle, Taveuni.

Copra drying, Bulia Island, Astrolabe lagoon, Kadavu.

Road through a copra plantation, Taveuni.

Taveuni is known as the garden isle of Fiji.

The famous and exclusive tagimoucea flower is found only at Taveuni and only above 600 metres on the mountain-side.

An aerial view of Sigatoka and another of Lautoka.

The township of Ba on the banks of the Ba River and surrounded by rich sugarcane fields.

The island of Bau which played such a significant role in Fiji's immediate past history.

A turtle on the beach of Turtle Island, in the Yasawa group.

Rainbow colours of the catamaran and lagoon at Beachcomber Island, Nadi
Bay being admired by two visitors from Australia.

An aerial view of Malolo Island from the north-west.

A panoramic view from the top of Sawa-i-lau island, Yasawa group.

Body-surfing, Natadola beach.

Luncheon at Castaway Resort, Mamanuca Islands.

The Island Express which services the resorts in the Mamanuca Islands.

Children playing on *bilibili,* a view from the Kings Road, Viti Levu.

An aerial view of Malolo Lailai.

A view from the top of Turtle Island, Yasawa group.

Sand dunes and coastline at the mouth of the Sigatoka River.

Sunset, Coral Coast.

Rewa ricefields near Nausori.

Canefields near Sigatoka.

River view, interior Viti Levu.

Hills and storm sky, interior Viti Levu.

Palm tree reflections, Coral Coast.

The beach at Vatukarasa, Coral Coast.

Nakelo landing, Rewa delta.

Fish traps on the Navaloa River, Rewa delta.

Sabeto canefields, Nadi.

Votua Levu, near the Nadi airport.

An aerial view of the reef and lagoon, Coral Coast.

A brilliant South Sea sunset.

Lagoon and islands near Ovalau, Lomaiviti.

Sunset, Natadola.

Navua River flats and small holdings.

Golf at Pacific Harbour. The course is one of the most attractive in the world and has been the venue for various national and international championships.

Beach such as dreams are made of — Yasawa Island, Yasawa group.

Prince Charles Beach, Taveuni.

A diver in the lagoon and his quarry.

Nadi Bay, staff leaving a resort hotel.

Fishing for prawns, Wainibuka River, Viti Levu.

Traditional village, interior Viti Levu.

Views from the interior, Viti Levu.

PRE HISTORY

The most remarkable aspect of Fijian pre-history is its antiquity. It is now known that people had reached the Fijian archipelago as early as 2000 years before the birth of Christ. Considering the fact that the Vikings, acknowledged as Europe's greatest sailors, didn't reach America until three thousand years later, or the fact that Columbus made his famous voyage only some five hundred years ago, the Fijian achievement must be seen as extraordinary.

The question is, who were the first settlers. And the answer is that we don't know. There are some who are prepared to speculate and Dr Roger Green, Professor of Anthropology at Auckland University, in New Zealand, is one of them. He has spent most of his academic career in trying to unravel this mystery and his broad theory is that a race of people entered the South Pacific from the Malay-Indonesian area. He calls this vast archipelago "Island South East Asia". These migrants were relatively new, even though they were moving in some 4000 years B.C. and their racial characteristics were different from those of the people already living in the islands of Papua New Guinea, the Solomon Islands, the Hebrides (now Vanuatu) and New Caledonia. The first settlers were of Negrito stock with dark skin, woolly hair and other typical features. The newcomers were fairer, had straight or wavy black hair and we can assume were of Malay type stock. They would seem to have been good sailors and craftsmen and excellent potters who made a distinct type of ware we know as Lapita pottery after its initial discovery in New Caledonia.

A picture emerges of these "Lapita" people. Sailors, adventurers, good navigators and consummate craftsmen. The trail of their pots, hooks, obsidian cutting tools and ornaments leads down from New Britain through some of the outer islands fringing the Solomons and Vanuatu, suggesting that perhaps they were not powerful enough to force settlements on the bigger islands which were already supporting large populations of people.

In this classic difference between the two groups we see the racial characteristics of what was later to be defined as Melanesian and Polynesian stock. The Melanesians were to retain their grip on the western islands of the South Pacific but it can be fairly assumed that a great deal of the "Lapita" blood found its way into its main stream.

At some stage, about 2000 years before the birth of Christ, a

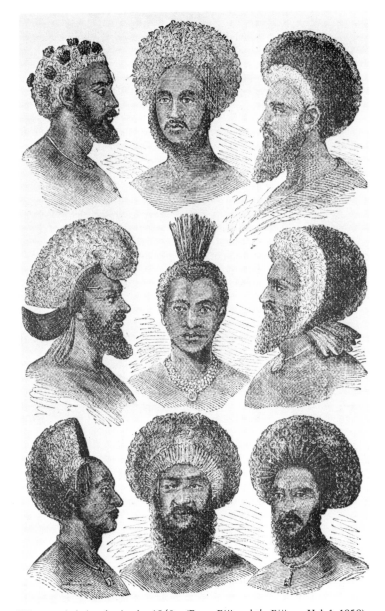

Fijian men's hairstyles in the 1840s. (From *Fiji and the Fijians*, Vol 1, 1858).

canoe load of venturesome "Lapita" sailors either deliberately set out to the east or were driven off course by a westerly wind and made landfall in the Fijian archipelago. Dr Green's theory is that these were the first settlers, not only because at that time they would have had the necessary maritime technology, but also be-

Levuka in 1838 from a lithograph based on a drawing by one of the artists accompanying the French navigator Dumont d'Urville
on the corvettes *l'Astrolabe* and *Zelee*.

cause their pottery is found throughout the whole of Fiji. There is no way of knowing how long they enjoyed Fiji to themselves. But at some stage the Melanesians followed. It is reasonable to suppose that groups of Melanesians who were in contact with the "Lapita" people in the west would have been quick to take advantage of the better craft used by the "Lapita" seafarers and

to incorporate these into their own technology.

It is also reasonable to assume that there may have been only a single successful voyage in each instance. Certainly Fijian legends speak of one canoe and one voyage. The canoe was the *Kaunitoni* and its people were the settlers. The legend says that the first canoe to touch land on the main island of Viti Levu

Naikorokoro, Ovalau, 1848. From a watercolour by Conway Shipley.

found an indigenous people. The legend also says that the people of the canoe made their way inland from where they eventually spilled to other parts of Fiji.

This would suggest that the most favourable coastal areas were already settled and that there was no room for the new arrivals, leaving them no choice but to move into the less hospitable interior, where over the ensuing generations their population built up and eventually spilled over.

We know who the Fijians are today, but we also know that they are not truly Melanesian when compared with what must have been the parent stock back in Vanuatu, the Solomon Islands or New Caledonia. The people of Fiji are larger — much larger in some cases, as in the province of Nadroga where even the women are nearly 180 centimetres (6 ft) tall. They speak a different language and enjoy their own material culture. At the time of European contact Fiji was a feudal society with a chiefly system of the most oppressive kind — unlike the Melanesian system where stature was earned by an individual who produced the most and shared it. In Fiji the chiefs had absolute power of life and death over commoners in contrast to the Melanesian system which opposed such tyranny.

We can try to imagine those first years. The canoe arriving, the hostile reception from the established population, the skirmishing and then the long trek into the interior; the build up of population and then the subsequent probing towards the coast for both peaceful and hostile interaction with the indigenous peoples.

"Women and land are the reasons men die," says an old Maori proverb and there is no reason to suppose it would have been different in pre-historic Fiji. Villages raided, men killed or enslaved and women taken as the prize of victory. Slowly the blood of the distinct ethnic groups would have diffused over both populations, but not to such an extent as to form a homogeneous whole. We can imagine two distinct groups, each modified by the blood of the other but each still retaining its distinct racial characteristics, building up to a series of greater confrontations until finally the descendents of the "Lapita" people are forced out, first into the eastern area of Fiji and then to Tonga and beyond, leaving the dominant Melanesian people in control until many centuries later when once again the descendents of the "Lapita" people, now known as Polynesians, would attempt to return and win back what they had lost.

The *kai Viti* — the people of Fiji — as they call themselves to this day, were left in possession of the large island archipelago which they began to organise on the Polynesian hierarchical system. Heads of powerful families could create political states by conquest and tyranny and by Machiavellian policies of alliance and treason. Friends and allies could become bitter enemies overnight. Political states, whose heads were often first cousins and sometimes step-brothers, were often locked in suicidal conflict. During greater wars minor civil wars would sometimes take place within political confederations and loyalty was something no Fijian chief could count on.

Fijians practised polygamy for both political and personal reasons. Alliances were consolidated by marriage, but women were also given as tribute or taken as a prize of war. The political advantage gained by marriage was often eroded by political instability at home caused by rivalry amongst the male issue. Thus families rose and fell and states rose and fell.

During this long pre-contact period Fiji was visited by Tongans who came on regular trading expeditions; Samoans, Wallis Islanders, people of Futuna and Rotuma. At some later stage, not long before European contact, there must also have been contact with Micronesia, most probably Kiribati 1100 miles to the north. The probability of such contact is beyond dispute because the development of the Fijian sailing canoe is so obviously based on the Micronesian model.

In 1976 I made such a voyage myself in a sailing canoe built at Tarawa, Kiribati. To my mind, it is more likely that a Micronesian canoe arrived in Fiji rather than a Fijian canoe arriving at Kiribati.

The famous English navigator/explorer James Cook notes the difference between the large voyaging canoes he saw in Tonga during his first visit in 1769. During his two subsequent calls he was able to note that the Fijian model had almost completely displaced the indigenous Tongan craft.

It was at Tonga that Cook first learned of Fiji and saw Fijian visitors who were conspicuous amongst the locals because of their darker skin. The Tongans maintained an intricate social relationship with Fiji through trade, through the supply of mercenary warriors to warring chiefdoms and through ancient rituals such as, for example the daughter of the Tui Tonga being reserved in marriage to the Tui Lakeba as she was considered too sacred for marriage to a Tongan. It would seem that Tongans were by far the most frequent visitors to Fiji because of the large material resources of Fiji. The Tongans came for sandalwood which was used for its scent and for the great double canoes which were so difficult to acquire in Tonga because of the lack of suitable timber. In turn the Tongans brought their own trade goods and their arms which they sold to the highest bidder and on whose behalf they would fight.

The Tongans could fish profitably in such waters, particularly in the period immediately after the first European contact when they came close to controlling most of Fiji and probably would have done so if it had not been for European intervention.

As the Fijians had no written language and relied on memory

for their history, (the wise men memorizing intricate genealogical tables), we have no record of what happened. Potsherds, hooks and artefacts unearthed in archaeological excavations are our only clue to the dim and distant past.

These show settlement of Fiji to have been achieved some four thousand years ago whereas today most Fijian people trace their descent through some ten generations to the landing of the canoe the *Kaunitoni* and the chiefs Lutunasobasoba and Degei. The canoe is said to have landed at Vuda between Lautoka and Nadi where Lutunasobasoba chose to remain. Others moved towards the Ra coast and settled on the seaward slopes of the Kauvadra range. Degei, who was subsequently deified, had numerous sons. They quarrelled and with their followers moved over much of Fiji until they finally settled, took wives from among the local people and founded the families that grew into the present chiefly *yavusa* recognised to this day. The *yavusa* is the largest social unit of the Fijians. According to R. A. Derrick in his *History of Fiji* (Government Press, Suva, 1946), a *yavusa* is strictly neither a tribe nor a clan; its members are direct agnate descendants of a single *kalou-vu* or deified ancestor; the unit originating from the Lutunasobasoba migration.

If the founder of the family had only one son the *yavusa* retained its patriarchal structure, even after his death, when in accordance with Polynesian custom his son succeeded him. If his family included two or more sons, the chiefly succession was from brother to brother and on the death of the last brother it reverted to the eldest son of the senior brother who had left male issue. Each member of the first such family of brothers founded a branch of the *yavusa* called a *mataqali* which thereafter retained its identity, acquired a distinctive name and in the course of time became the traditional custodian of a designated function. In a fully developed *yavusa* there was *mataqali*: 1, the *turaga* or chiefly *mataqali,* who were in the most direct line of descent, by male links, from the common ancestor, and from whom the ruling chiefs of succeeding generations were chosen; 2, the *sauturaga* or executive *mataqali,* whose rank was next to that of the chiefs of the blood and whose function it was to carry out their commands and to support their authority; 3, the *mata-ni-vanua* or diplomatic *mataqali,* from whom the official heralds and masters of ceremony were chosen; 4, *bete* or priestly *mataqali,* into certain of whom the spirit of the common ancestor was supposed to enter

and 5, the *bati* or warrior *mataqali* whose function was war. The third and smallest unit was the *i tokatoka* which was a subdivision of the *mataqali* and comprised closely relating families acknowledging the same blood relative as their head and living in a defined village area.

The simple branching of *yavusa* into *mataqali* and of the *mataqali* into the *i tokatoka* was subject to disruptive influences of war, internal strife, migration and conquest. This was a dynamic process subject to internal and external stress which saw many of the original *yavusa* broken or merged wholly or in part with others forming new groups called *vanua* each under a paramount chief strong enough to seize and hold the position which thereafter became hereditary. Some of the *vanua* were united by conquest or accretion into kingdoms known as *matanitu*. But this is regarded as a recent development during the wars of historic times. Among the people of the interior and western Viti Levu large confederations were unknown. In 1835 the people of Fiji said there were thirty-two places in the group entitled to rank as *matanitu,* but during the British Colonial period the Native Lands Commission found the political status and order of precedence of the chiefdoms to be as follows: Bau, Rewa, Naitasiri, Namosi, Nadroga, Bua, Macuata, Cakaudrove, Lau, Kadavu, Ba, Serua and Tavua. The life of Fijians was governed by ritual accompanied by elaborate ceremonies and strict observance of ancient custom. A serious breach of etiquette or error in precedence could lead to bloodshed or even war. There is a recorded instance of the chief of Rewa inviting his *bati* (warriors) from different parts of his state to a feast in their honour. Whereas in the past the numerous companies had been honoured separately, on this occasion the chief decided to bring them together but a dispute quickly arose over precedence between two parties and neither would yield and determined to settle the issue with the club. The chiefs of Rewa, fearing that once started such a disturbance could lead to a greater conflict, promptly fired muskets on the disturbing parties.

There were appropriate ceremonies for every event of importance and also for many minor ones. Life was governed by superstitious beliefs. Good and evil fortune was ascribed to the will of gods and spirits which needed to be constantly propitiated with gifts but especially the presentation of the bodies of slain victims which would then be redistributed for cooking and eating. Major

Portraits of Fijian chiefs.

events such as the installation of great chiefs were sometimes conducted over a pile of bodies and the birth, coming of age, marriage and death of great chiefs were likely to be marked with human sacrifice as were the stages in the buildings of war canoes — and especially their launching which was over the bodies of live victims tied down over the skids — and the setting up of the principal posts for temples or chiefs' houses when live men would be buried to "hold them up". On such occasions the ceremonial preparation and serving of *yaqona* was an important part of the ritual as was the presentation of the *tabua*. In recent times the name *tabua* has come to signify the tooth of the sperm whale. In former times it was a special stone cut and polished in the shape of a sperm whale tooth, but larger in size, which was used. The incidence of whaling ships in the Pacific during the nineteenth century caused a large supply of whale teeth to become available. At first these were introduced into Fiji by Tongans who had a better access to them, but later European trading ships brought these directly. *Tabua* were the price of life and death and indispensable adjuncts to every proposal, whether for marriage, alliance, intrigue, request, apology, appeal to the gods or sympathy with the bereaved. Priests were an important link between the gods and the people but the gods were capricious and, even if there was proper observance of all customary rites and the presentation of suitable gifts, the god or gods could still with-

hold their favour. At such times an explanation might be demanded of the priests and on some occasions the gods have been challenged to fight.

Degei, the deified ancestor of the Lutunasobasoba migration, was recognised as the most important. He is said to have lived (in pre-Christian times) near the place of his original settlement following the landing of the canoe at Vuda and his march to the Kauvadra Range. Degei became a huge snake living in a cave on the mountain Uluda. No cave has been found on the summit of Uluda, but there is a cleft hardly wide enough for a man to fit into. There were gods of agriculture, fishing, craftsmen and war.

The god of war often received the greatest attention because so much depended on him. No campaign was begun without his temple being either completely rebuilt or refurbished and the presentation of lavish gifts. The *bure kalou* (the temple), of which two fine examples may be seen in Fiji today at Pacific Harbour and at Orchid Island near Suva, was the home of the god. The temples were built on high platforms of stone and earth and were marked by lofty roofs which dominated all others, including the elaborate houses of the highest chiefs. The interior was beautifully decorated with sennit and cowerie shells. A strip of *masi* cloth hung from the roof framing and descended to the floor where it was draped before a corner post. It was down this curtain that the god would descend when invoked.

Club dance at Levuka performed in honour of the officers of the U.S. Exploring Expedition, 1840. (From C. Wilkes, 1854, Narrative of the United States Exploring Expedition, 1838–1842).

Because Fijians believed in the power of gods and spirits and in sorcery, the office of the priest was important. Priests were the link between gods and men and for this important function they received gifts for the use of the gods, but in reality appropriated by the priests. The ritual in seeking the god's favour centred on the preparation of a feast which would be presented in the temple along with an offering of the *tabua*. All would then sit silently in the cool, gloomy interior of the *bure kalou* and gaze with expectation on the priest who would sit before the strip of *masi* along which the god would be expected to descend. The priest would begin to twitch until finally he would be in a fit with violent convulsions, sweat running out of every pore and frothing at the

Interior of a temple at Levuka 1838. Lithograph based on a drawing by one of the artists accompanying Dumont d'Urville.

mouth. In this state the priest was in the possession of the god and he would speak to the assembly in a strange voice, often ambiguously, until he would cease to shake when it was recognised that the god had departed. Much depended on what the god promised. If success, all was jubilation but if it was failure, not even the boldest chiefs would dare move. The feast and gifts offered to the god would then be shared by the priests and petitioners. Only the spirit substance of the gifts would be used by the god.

The Fijians believed in an afterlife. This was an island somewhere to the west from where the original migration (migrations) had come. The path taken by the soul was always difficult and frought with dangers. Evil spirits awaited the traveller; some needed gifts while others had to be fought and prevailed against

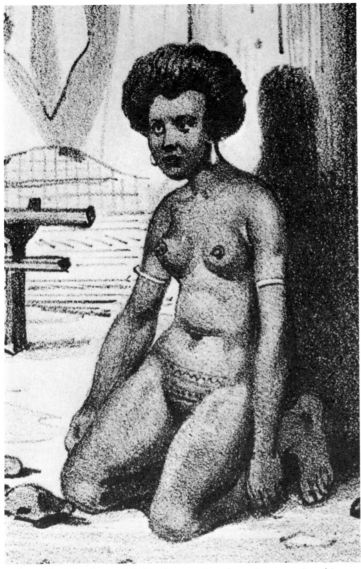

A detail from the former. Notice the tattooing about the woman's pubic area. Fiji girls had to be tattooed about the genitals and loins before they could be initiated as women. As women were strictly barred from temples, it seems that these may have been brought there for the benefit of the visiting Frenchmen.

without some consequence. Illness or death was attributed to the action of sorcery; to the breaking of the *tabu* or to the displeasure of the gods. The Fijian also believed in the importance of dreams and omens and in the power of spells to such an extent that if informed of a death spell he would be likely to die unless relief could be obtained by a more potent spell. Some omens were extremely powerful — the sight of a kingfisher was sufficient to send a war-party into a retreat.

Chiefs held absolute power over their subjects and could have them killed at will. The strictest laws of *tabu* applied to the protection of the privilege enjoyed by chiefs. Commoners and women had to move out of the path of chiefs, kneel, clap their hands and greet him with a cry of respect. In passing his presence they had to stoop or even sometimes crawl; if carrying objects these had to be lowered; when entering the house in his presence the commoner had to use a door reserved for him. The power of chiefs was demonstrated in the 1840s by a chief of Rewa. An American trader who had purchased the Island of Laucala near the mouth of the Rewa River had requested the chief to stop people from going to it. A canoe load of the chief's subjects, unaware of the prohibition, was seen on its way to the island. The chief immediately sent warriors who clubbed the unfortunates to death. The largest chiefdoms were the most oppressive tyrannies.

The artistic feeling of the Fijians was expressed in the construction of the great war canoes; in the building and decoration of temples and chiefs houses; in the decoration of weapons, cloth, pottery and in the intricate and colourful decoration of the person. The *meke,* a combination of song and dance, are popular to this day whilst the proper execution of ceremonies and rituals, such as the serving of the chief's *yaqona* and the presentation of the *tabua,* were dramatic events.

Until the coming of Europeans, the Fijian craftsman worked with stone tools and his achievements, when seen in this light must be regarded with credit. With these tools he built great canoes and houses for the chiefs and gods. The house of Tanoa at Bau was 40 metres long and 13 metres wide and that of his son, Cabokabu was 24 metres long, 11 metres wide and 12 metres high. The huge posts, some of which were nearly two metres in circumference, were felled in the bush and then hauled by manpower to the sea, brought to Bau and then manhandled again to the site of construction. It was in the construction of the great

so that the soul might continue on its path. Those who were unsuccessful were eaten. It could be said that the world of the Fijian was completely bound by superstition and ritual and sorcery. Every action could bring gain or harm. Nothing could be done

Fijian chiefs. (From *Fiji and the Fijians*, Vol 1, 1858).

war canoes that the art of the Fijian craftsman was revealed. Two examples (on a small scale) may be seen in Fiji today. One is in the Fiji Museum at Suva and the other at Orchid Island near Suva. The canoe at the museum was built in the early 1900s and is a fine example of exquisite craftsmanship. It is truly a work of art. The difference in the work of the time when the canoe was built and now can be seen readily in the restoration work which seems crude in comparison with the original. But both canoes are small in comparison with the great craft which ruled the seas during much of the 19th century. The greatest fleet was assembled at Bau where some of these craft were of unbelievable size. The famous *Ra Marama,* which was built at Taveuni, was nearly 32 metres long and more than 5.6 metres wide. It took seven years to build it. Such canoes not only required the expertise of crafts-

Fijian chiefs, study in decoration. (From Caines Jannif archives.)

men but the resources of great states. It is difficult to imagine, for example, how many kilometres of sennit (coconut husk cord) would have to be made for the lashings which would hold the various parts of the canoe together. My own estimate, based on the outrigger canoe built at Tarawa, Kiribati, in 1975–76 which we sailed down to Fiji, would suggest that upwards of ten thousand metres of sennit would be required if rigging was included in the total.

The art of pottery brought into the South Pacific by the gifted and versatile "Lapita" people survived in Fiji but failed in Tonga, Samoa and east Polynesia on account of the lack of suitable clay. The Fijians still make pottery and it is possible to join a tour to a village in Sigatoka where the art is demonstrated. But the pottery of recent historic times has degenerated considerably from the ware made by the first settlers. It was an important trade item carried to Tonga and Samoa and on at least one occasion, possibly by the only canoe to make such a voyage, as far as the Marquesas Islands more than two thousand nautical miles to the east. As throughout the rest of the South Pacific, cloth was made from the paper-mulberry tree. The craft is practised to this day and may be seen in the Lau Islands and especially at Taveuni. The trees are specially cultivated in groves. When about four metres high and some three centimetres in diameter the trees are harvested and the skin removed for processing. This is done by first steeping it in water and then by scraping and beating until the desired texture is achieved. This cloth is known as *masi* in Fiji but is also called *tapa*. Much of it is directed at the tourist trade as a curiosity, but it is also used by Fijians as a dress for ceremonial occasions. In former times there were many regional styles of decoration. It is hard to imagine the people of those times being afflicted by "unemployment" and it is sometimes difficult to imagine that this can be so today. Houses need constant attention and repair; there were ropes and nets and mats to be made; weapons, utensils of every kind, fish hooks from bone and shell and wood, needles, slit gongs large and small, canoes of all kinds, combs and ornaments and huge plantations to maintain and harvest, the surplus being laid down in special pits to ferment and congeal into a paste which would last for years.

The best of all the labour of craftsmen, gardeners and fishermen was enjoyed by the chiefs.

Re-enactment of a raiding party bringing back a corpse for the cannibal oven. The men wear the traditional *masi* cloth *malo* and carry a wide variety of clubs. (Caines Jannif archives photo.)

CANNIBALISM

The Fijians were fierce cannibals. This fact is so well documented that there can be no argument. The Fijians have no explanation for their eating of human flesh other than to say that it was the "custom of the land". There is also no account and no legend of how the custom began except that it started on the island of Gau.

However, it is unlikely that Gau was the origin of cannibalism in Fiji as the eating of human flesh was practised throughout the South Pacific in both Melanesia and Polynesia. Marco Polo, during his voyage from China to Persia at the close of the 13th century, described attacks on his people in Sumatra and says these were made by cannibals. The Fijians ranked with the best,

128

such as the people of the Marquesas Islands and the Maori of New Zealand. There were hundreds and possibly thousands of people killed and eaten between the time of European contact at the beginning of the 1800s and the signing of the deed of cession of Fiji to Britain in 1874. Within that total, at least 100 Europeans were killed and eaten during this time, the last being the Reverend Baker who was killed and eaten in the interior of Viti Levu in 1868. The Wesleyan Missionaries who were the first to attempt to convert Fijians to Christianity began their mission in 1935 and are, for the most part, the most reliable source of information of cannibalism because they were unwilling witness to it. Thus, in 1849 the missionaries at Rewa were "awakened by strange noises on the other side of the river. On running out they saw for the first time the horrid sight of the dragging of human bodies, seventeen of which were just being handed out of a canoe, having been sent from Mabu as the Rewa share of two hundred and sixty people killed in the sacking of towns belonging to Verata. One of the corpses was that of an old man of seventy, another of a fine young woman of eighteen, the others being youths and strong men. All were dragged about and subjected to abuse too horrible and disgusting to be described, and the sight of which gave the terrified spectators across the river such a shock as they did not get over for many days." And great was the jealousy of high chiefs as shown by the classic example of Qaraniqio, one of the principal men of Rewa. On hearing that a young woman reserved for him on the island of Kadavu had been unfaithful with a chief of Nakasaleka village, he sailed across with a large force and burnt the town, killing and causing many of the people to be eaten. The accused chief and other survivors escaped to a mountain stronghold and refused to come down until the young chief finally volunteered to go down and die in order to save the rest. A companion of the chief insisted upon accompanying him in order that they might die together. On reaching the shore the two sat down. The chiefs of Rewa and their warriors were assembled and an oven was already being prepared, the fire burning over the hot stones, in which the two hapless victims were soon cooked and eaten. The woman was taken back to Rewa where it was found that she was still a virgin and that the report of her unfaithfulness had been raised by a party who had a grievance with the people of Nakasaleka.

In 1843, at what was to mark the start of hostilities between Rewa and Bau, a village where Government House now stands was taken and more than 100 people killed and eaten. The survivors fled to a fortress at Tamavua where they were once again attacked and this time all of them were destroyed and eaten.

It was not only enemies who were killed and eaten as this incident will illustrate. The Butoni tribe was composed of expert sea rovers who went about exacting tribute on behalf of Bau. In 1849 they arrived at Bau with a large offering of property. Custom demanded they be fed *bokola* — human flesh — and two young men were killed and served.

The chief of the Lasakau tribe, Gavidi, whose function it was to procure bodies for cannibal feasts gathered his priests and announced: "We shall lose our renown. We shall not be dreaded or fed. We have provided no food for our visitors. We will seek for enemies of Bau. If we cannot catch any enemies, we will kill some who are friendly and if we cannot get either friends or enemies, some of our own must be strangled." The expedition set out in a number of canoes and after lying in wait fell upon fourteen women and one man. The women were taken alive and the man was killed on the spot. News of the capture was brought to Bau and reached the adjoining island of Viwa where the wives of two missionaries were residing alone; their husbands away on other islands. With great trepidation but unshakable purpose, the two immediately set out to Bau. As they approached "the din of the cannibals grew louder." The account as published in the *History of the Mission in Fiji* by James Calvert continues: "The death-drum sounded terrible and muskets were fired in triumph. Then, as they came nearer, shriek after shriek pierced through every other noise, and told that the murder was begun. Fear gave way to impatience at that wild warning, and the Englishwomen's voices urged the labouring boatmen to make better speed. They reached the beach and were met by a *lotu* (Christian) chief, who dared to join them saying, 'Make haste! Some are dead; but some are alive!' Surrounded by an unseen guard which none might break through, the women of God passed among the blood maddened cannibals unhurt. They pressed forward to the house of the old king, Tanoa, the entrance to which was strictly forbidden to all women. It was no time for ceremony now. With a whale's tooth in each hand, and still accompanied by the Christian chief, they thrust themselves into the grim presence of the King, and prayed their prayer of mercy. The old man was startled at the audacity of the intruders. His hearing was dull, and they raised their voices higher to plead for their dark sisters' lives. The King said, 'Those who are dead are dead; but those who are still alive shall live only.' At that word, a man ran to Gavidi, to stop his butchery, and returned to say that five still lived; the rest of the fourteen were killed."

The principal temple of Bau was *Vata ni Tawake* which has been rebuilt again in facsimile, but with modern materials. It stands today as a reminder of the past and no doubt to some, the former glory and power of Bau where once the hundreds of corpses of its enemies and victims were thrown as votive offerings, from where they were be apportioned by the Roko Tui Bau to those who would eat them. In August 1848 H.M.S. *Havannah* arrived in Fiji and its Captain was taken by the missionaries on a visit to Bau. He described his visit: "The building [of the temple] stood on a raised platform, and was surrounded by a few trees of graceful foliage, under one of which lay the large wooden *lali,* or sacred drum, beaten at festivals and sacrifices; and overshadowed by another was the place where bodies of victims were dedicated to the *kalou,* or evil spirit, previous to their being handed to those who are to cook them for the banquet. The lower branches of the tree had evidently been lately cut away to the height of eight or ten feet from the ground; and we were told that this had been done after the reduction of *Lokia,* a town belonging to Rewa, a few months before, when a mound of no fewer than eighty corpses slain in battle, had been heaped up on the spot.

"We came at last," the Captain continued, "upon an irregular square, on which stood a building, probably 100 feet long, the 'stranger's' house', still occupied by the Butoni people, and we entered it by a door in the centre. The interior struck me at first as resembling the lower deck of a ship of war, there being a passage down the centre, and the families living in separate messes on either side; divided, however, from each other, in some cases by partitions of coloured native cloth. We met the usual welcome from the people who happened to be there, and several of them followed our party out, through an opposite door to that by which we had entered, to a small level space between the back of the house and the hill, which rises somewhat abruptly behind. The first objects of interest to which our attention was called by these strangers, as if to vaunt the goodness of their reception in

A young boy about to be circumcised with a bamboo knife in an initiation rite. (Caines Jannif archive photo.)

the capital, were four or five ovens, loosely filled in with stones, which had served to cook the human bodies presented to them after the payment of their tribute. They certainly did not understand the expressions of disgust which rose to our lips; for leading

A romantic view of a Fijian maiden. (Caines Jannif archives photo.)

us to a neighbouring tree, they pointed to where, suspended from the branches, hung some scraps of flesh, the remains of the wretched creatures slaughtered to satisfy the monstrous appetite of these fellows, who had not even the miserable excuse of enmity or hunger to plead for their fiendish banquet."

In 1853 Cakobau was installed as the *Vunivalu* of Bau. The Wesleyan missionary James Calvert, who was in residence on the nearby island of Viwa, was informed that 18 persons of the Nakelo tribe had just been taken to Bau, some dead and some alive. He at once went to Bau and learned that of the 18 one had escaped, twelve were dead and five still alive. On reaching the temples at Lasakau and Soso [that part of Bau reserved for these tribes] a fearful sight presented itself to the missionary. The mangled bodies of the dead were exposed there, and the survivors, bound and badly wounded, looked at the white man with intense anxiety. He at once went to Cakobau who refused to interfere. Calvert describes how he went from Cakobau to the Tui Cakau, whose men had taken the victims and back again to the chief of the Lasakau but in vain. As he approached "the great temple *Vata ni Tawaki* a dead stillness rested upon Bau, which was suddenly broken by a loud shout, proclaiming that Cakobau had just drunk the *yaqona* of the Vunivalu, during the preparation of which none were allowed to move about. Another shout from the Lasakau quarter made known that the bodies were being dragged; and soon the horrible procession came up — the

A Fijian girl in traditional dress. The brevity of her *liku* skirt shows she has not been tattooed or initiated as a woman. If so, she would wear a skirt which completely encircled the hips and buttocks. Girls were usually tattooed and initiated as women at puberty, but those of high rank often not until their late teens.

dead and the dying, dragged along by their hands, naked, with their heads rattling and grating over the rough ground. As each approached the temple, the head was violently dashed against a great stone, which became stained with blood."

Peter Dillon, an English seaman, was also an unwilling witness to a cannibal feast in which, but for his quick thinking, he would surely have been a victim. It happened in Vanua Levu when a number of Europeans had joined a Bauan army in a mercenary expedition. Among them was the infamous Charles Savage, whose deadly aim had so much helped the rise of Bau. The army of more than two hundred men marched up the hillside and burnt a village, thinking that the local people had fled. Instead they had laid a careful ambush and within minutes eighty Bauans and several Europeans were dead. Dillon, Savage and several others fought their way to the coast where they found their way barred by hundreds of warriors. They fought their way up a steep rock which to this day is known as Dillon's Rock and there made a stand with Dillon, Savage and another designated marksman, shooting at their attackers while the others reloaded. The attackers lost many men and soon realised it would be too costly to drag the Europeans off the rock. Instead they left them to roast in the sun and the beleaguered group, with no drinking water and diminishing stocks of ammunition, were in a desperate state. After some time, following the cessation of hostilities, Charles Savage and a Chinaman decided to go down and bargain for their lives. Dillon insisted they leave their guns and ammunition and then reluctantly allowed them to go. As Savage and the Chinaman reached the Fijians only a hundred metres or so from the rock, the Chinaman and Savage were separated and the Fijians, pretending friendship, tried to get the others down. When they saw that Dillon and his men would not descend, the Chinaman was clubbed and Savage seized and his head held in a pool of water until he was dead. Their bodies, along with those of the other Europeans and Bauans killed in the battle, were cut up and placed in the ovens and cooked before Dillon and his men. During this time the Fijians described in graphic detail that this would soon be the fate of Dillon and his party. In the event Dillon and his men cheated the oven by taking hostage one of the high priests of Wailea and marching him, with their guns at his head, through the centre of the Fijian army to a ship's boat waiting for them just off shore.

WIDOW STRANGLING

Just as abhorrent to the Europeans was the Fijian custom of strangling wives on the death of their husbands. As great chiefs had many wives, this could be a grisly affair. The custom was so ingrained that it could be used in reverse. For example, when a chief of Bau was killed by his own people his wife was not strangled to accompany him to give his spirit the satisfaction of having her in the next life. The distraught woman tried desperately to kill herself but was restrained and it was only some weeks later when she accepted Christianity that she gave up the idea of doing away with herself. But not all wives were so eager. On the death of the younger son of the Tui Cakau, who was lost in a canoe, 18 young women were strangled. Three wives of the Lasakau chief Gavidi were strangled and Cakobau proposed to strangle his own sister but the Lasakau people begged for her life as she was pregnant and they wanted the child for their new chief. In her stead the dead chief's mother had offered herself and the offer was accepted. A servant was also killed. It was Cakobau himself who had pulled on the strangling cord which killed Gavidi's mother.

The most graphic account of strangling is given by James Calvert on the death of Tanoa at Bau. As Tanoa weakened, the missionaries made every effort to secure the release of his wives from death but Cakobau would not accede and instead urged the missionary to go and see the women whom the missionaries found resolved to die. On December 7th one of the missionaries, Watsford, went to Bau alone, Calvert having been called away to Ovalau. He found an assembly of women at Tanoa's house. They were weeping over those selected to die. At Cakobau's house he was still more shocked to see women preparing the dresses for the others to wear on the day of their death. Tanoa died during the night and early next morning Watsford returned to Bau and, hurrying to the house where the body lay, he saw six biers standing at the door and he thus knew that at least five women had been selected to follow their lord to the grave. Calvert described the scene thus:

"Within the house the work of death was begun. One woman was already strangled, and the second was kneeling with covered head, while several men on either side were just pulling the cord which wound around her neck, when the missionary stood on the threshold, heart-sick and faint at the ghastly sight. Soon the

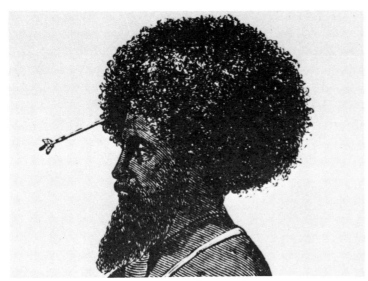

Seru Cakobau, son of Tanoa, Vunivalu of Bau, 1849.

woman fell dead. Mr Watsford knew her. She had professed christianity, and shrunk from death, asking to go to prayer. But when the fatal moment came, she rose when called, and, passing the old king's corpse, spat on it saying, 'Ah, you old wretch! I shall be in hell with you directly!' The third was now called for, when Cakobau caught sight of the missionary, and, trembling with fear, looked at him in agony, and cried out, 'What about it, Mr Watsford?' Mr Watsford with great difficulty answered, 'Refrain, Sir! That is plenty. Two are dead. Refrain — I love them!' The chief replied, 'We also love them. They are not many — only five. But for you missionaries, many more would have been strangled.' Just then the third victim approached, who had offered to die instead of her sister, who had a son living. She had sat impatiently; and on hearing her name started instantly. She was a fine woman, of high rank, and wore a new *liku* [skirt]. Looking proudly round on the people seated in the apartment, she pranced up to the place of death, offering her hand to Mr Watsford, who shrunk back in disgust. When about to kneel, she saw that they were going to use a shabby cord, and haughtily refused to be strangled, except with a new cord. All this time the assembly gazed at her with delight, gently clapping their hands, and expressing, in subdued exclamations, their admiration for her beauty and pride. She then bid her relatives farewell, and knelt down, with her arms round one of her friends. The cord was

Tanoa Visawaqa, Vunivalu of Bau, 1840. (From C. Wilkes, 1845. Narrative of the U.S. Exploring Expedition, 1838–1842.)

adjusted, and the large covering thrown over her; and while the men strained the cord, a lady of rank pressed down on the head of the poor wretch, who died without sound or struggle. Two more followed. Throughout the terrible scene there was no noise of excitement; but a cheerful composure seemed to possess everyone there, except Cakobau, who was much excited, and evidently making a great effort to act his murderous part before the face of God's messenger. He ordered that one of the victims should live; but she refused; and her son helped the King and the rest to strangle her."

Calvert concludes the description: "So died Tanoa, Vunivalu and Chief of Bau, and such were the obsequies of the man who that day had ended an unusually long life, throughout which he had been an unchanged cannibal; and he perished in his sins."

THE RISE OF BAU

As elsewhere in the Pacific, European contact precipitated a series of crises which profoundly disturbed the world of the native peoples. In Fiji the small island state of Bau which at the time was expanding its power was the first to put the mercenary capacity of the shipwrecked Charles Savage to use. He soon demonstrated his deadly aim in the Rewa delta where he shot most of the inhabitants of a village and then again in the sacking of Verata. Savage and several others were survivors from the wreck of the American brig *Eliza* on Mocea reef in 1808. The ship was ostensibly coming to Fiji for sandalwood, but no explanation can be found for the fact that it carried 40,000 Spanish gold dollars, or the large stock of arms and ammunition. The ship struck the reef in calm weather and the crew had no difficulty in salvaging most of the money. They took 34,000 of the gold coins into a longboat along with navigational instruments, muskets, powder and ball, cutlasses and some of their clothes. They reached the nearby island of Nairai and buried the money but the Fijians were quickly on the scene and stripped the castaways of everything, including the clothes they wore. Within a week the captain and four others were allowed to leave in the longboat for Sandalwood Bay, taking with them 6000 dollars which they had managed to recover. A further 9000 were traded back, while two of the crew, Patterson and Steere, got away with a few more and eventually reached Sandalwood Bay and the safety of the ships lying there. But Charlie Savage went to Bau while four of his more desperate companions went to Verata. The Vunivalu of Bau, Naulivou, was given an expert demonstration of Charlie's aim and the deadly power of the gun against those armed with clubs and spears.

The Bauan war party took him to Kasavu, a village on the Rewa River where he shot so many that the survivors built a wall from the corpses as the only means of their preservation. The Fijians said that Charlie was never known to miss. Before the attack on Verata, Savage warned his friends and the four shipmates fled to Bau. Others, drawn by tales of the lost Spanish dollars found their way to the island to swell its ranks of mercenaries. Soon there were twenty of them. They were the instrument of terror of Naulivou and in turn they were pampered and rewarded with status normally only accorded to chiefs. They were given women of rank for their wives and lavish gifts of food and property. Some of their number fell through violence caused by dissention among themselves and the four men from Verata were clubbed when they caused a disturbance over the division of a feast. Savage was undoubtedly the most renowned and the most feared among them. He was given the daughter of the Roko Tui Bau for his wife and numerous other women of lesser rank. But only his daughters were allowed to live, the male issue being killed at birth to avoid future dynastic problems. During his short term of five years in Bau it is probable he killed more than five hundred men, until his own death and ignominious end in a Fijian oven. The Bauan state, thus expanded, was inherited by Tanoa, the father of Cakobau — the man who was to have the most profound effect on Fiji.

Tanoa's oppressive rule was broken by a coup in the 1830s but Tanoa escaped in a canoe, being pursued by the Chief of Viwa, Namosimalua. When Tanoa reached the island of Nairai, Namosimalua, instead of immediately attacking him in the village where he was resting, delayed action and assured his crew there would be ample time the next day. That night he sent a secret message to Tanoa and in the morning Tanoa was well on his way to Somosomo on the island of Taveuni. Namosimalua had urged the death of Cakobau, marking in him the qualities which could prove dangerous to those who had caused his father to lose power. As Cakobau was only one of many male issue by different women and seemed to have no political interest, he was allowed to live. But Cakobau was secretly planning his revenge and in league with Namosimalua's nephew Varani, he made his counter move. One morning Bau woke to find a pallisade had been erected around the rebel quarter and their houses fired before the attack. Many of the rebel chiefs were killed and others taken prisoner, but those who managed to escape were eventually given up by those who gave them shelter. Tanoa was brought back in style and had the satisfaction of having one of the leaders of the rebellion brought before his presence where he had his tongue ripped out and ate it before the eyes of his victim. But despite Cakobau's repeated request, Tanoa refused to have Namosimalua killed, much to the amazement of others who could not understand his leniency.

With the coup, Cakobau — the name given to him for his bold stroke and meaning, in some interpretations, the man who burned Bau — assumed supreme executive power of the Vunivalu leaving his father as the figurehead. He soon stamped the force of his personality on the politics of the islands and without doubt impressed himself as the most wilful, intelligent and energetic of the chiefs of his time. Only one man, Maafu the Tongan, would pose a serious challenge. He was inordinately ambitious and though clinging to Fijian custom, this was only to serve him in his aim of winning by conquest and intrigue the title of *Tui Viti* (the King of Fiji) which he so desperately wanted.

A vivid description of Cakobau is given by Captain Erskine, of H.M.S. *Havannah* during his visit in 1849.

"We arrived at last at the residence of Cakobau himself, and here we were received with much ceremony. An entrance having been cleared for us through bundles of native cloth, immense coils of cordage, and other articles, the produce of the late visit of the Butoni tribe, the chief himself — the most powerful, perhaps of any in the Pacific, and certainly the most energetic in character — was seen seated in the attitude of respect to receive us. He rose, however, as we entered, seeing that it was expected, unfolding, as he did so, an immense train of white native cloth, eight or ten yards long, from his waist and invited me to occupy the one chair he possessed; the others taking their seats on the rolls of cloth, or, like the natives, sitting cross-legged on the floor. It was impossible but to admire the appearance of the Chief: of large, almost gigantic size, his limbs were beautifully formed and proportioned; his countenance, with far less of the Negro cast than among the lower orders, agreeable and intelligent; while his immense head of hair, covered and concealed with gauze, smoke dried and slightly tinged with brown, gave him altogether the appearance of an eastern sultan. No garments confined his magnificent chest and neck, or concealed the natural colour of the skin, a clear but decided black; and in spite of his paucity of attire — the evident wealth which surrounded him showing that it was a matter of choice and not of necessity — he looked every inch a King. The missionaries said he was a little agitated with the prospect of an interview, but I confess I did not discover it. Not far from him sat his principal and favourite wife, a stout good-looking woman with a smiling expression, and her son Cakobau's heir, a fine boy of eight or nine; and he was surrounded at a respectful distance by a crowd of crouching courtiers.'

This was the man who was to have such an inordinate sway on Fiji and who, more than any other, would be responsible for the cession of Fiji to Britain in 1874, and it would be one of his descendants, Ratu George Cakobau who would become the first Governor-General of the newly independent nation.

On assuming power, Cakobau seemed set to enjoy it without any obvious urgent need to extend the power of Bau. In the face of the most extreme provocation from Rewa which caused Suva to be destroyed and its inhabitants eaten, he chose to ignore it and took himself off to Lakeba in Lau where he stayed for several months. There were many reasons why he was reluctant to seek confrontation: his father had been given asylum at Rewa during his exile; Tanoa's mother was a woman of the highest rank in Rewa and the two states had been in a close and most amicable relationship. When Cakobau returned he found the situation worse. Tanoa's principal wife and the mother of Cakobau's half-brother Rivalita, had been unfaithful and had run away to Rewa taking with her several women from Tanoa's household. Instead of being sent back, these women were given to different chiefs of Rewa, thus offering the worst possible insult to Bau. Tanoa forgot the help given him during his exile and war was declared, the Bauan party immediately gaining an advantage by splitting Rewa by gaining the allegiance of one of the brothers of the principal chief. This man, who had assumed the English name of Phillips after a visit to America, was promised the chiefdom of Rewa as soon as the Bauans killed the ruling chief and another brother, Qaraniqio. The Bauans, helped by Phillips, gained immediate ascension, burning and destroying many of the villages belonging to those loyal to the chief. At that time the death drum seldom ceased and the cannibal ovens were almost never empty. At one stage, just to introduce a variation, the Bauans threw 25 Rewans onto hot coals and roasted them alive. The Rewans pinned their hopes on Rivalita, the son of Tanoa and the sister of the Rewan chief and half-brother to Cakobau. He had conspired to kill Cakobau, take over his position and also assume the overlordship of Rewa. Cakobau had Rivalita killed in 1846. He was clubbed down and then buried alive, his cries audible from the hole where he had been thrown. The next disaster to fall on Rewa occurred when Cakobau pretened to accept an offer of submission of Rewa, but instead conspired to kill the principal chief. The Bauan canoes arrived to accept the surrender, but when the principal chief came out with his wife and children, he was ordered to go back into his town. He refused and was shot and clubbed before the eyes of his wife and family. At the same time conspirators set the town on fire and opened the gates to the Bauans. It is estimated that up to four hundred people were killed that day but Qaraniqio, who was not inside, escaped to continue the war. The body of the slain chief was taken to Bau and buried without the usual honours — no women or slaves strangled to accompany him to the grave. The jubilation of Bau was short-lived. They had achieved their goal, but only partially and Qaraniqio was still loose to menace them, while other events were taking their own shape.

The Europeans that Bau had used to its own advantage had now formed a presence of their own in Levuka on the island of Ovalau. The missionaries were now firmly established since their arrival in Fiji in 1835 and were gaining converts whose attitude to wars and the ancient Fijian customs of cannibalism and widow strangling were contrary to Cakobau's expectations. Bau was also involved on a much larger scale throughout, especially in eastern Fiji, where Lau, the domains of the Tui Cakau at Taveuni and Vanua Levu on the north-eastern coast, the chiefdoms of north-western Vanua Levu, the islands of Ovalau and Moturiki and the Ra coast, as far as Ba on Viti Levu, acknowledged the power of Bau with tributes of woman, canoes, food, sennit, cloth and men. Bau's authority, however, though acknowledged was not necessarily secure and there was yet another factor which, like the presence of whites, was to have a profound effect on Fijian politics. While Cakobau was consolidating his power over Rewa and Eastern Fiji the Tongan presence in Lau, based mainly in Lakeba, was growing.

In 1848 the high chief of Tonga, Enele Ma'afuotu'itoga, sub-

David Whippy, American adventurer, whose descendents number more than a thousand in Fiji today. A shipyard he founded in 1840 in Levuka still flourishes in Suva.

sequently known as Maafu, arrived in Fiji. The sudden appearance of European warships was an important factor. The French corvettes *Astrolabe* and *Zelee* destroyed the houses and plantations of Viwa in retaliation for the taking of the *l'Aimable Josephine*. An American warship took away a Rewan chief responsible for the death of American citizens. The Europeans introduced a series of epidemics against which the Fijians had no immunity and which severely reduced the population of the group.

The astute political management of Bau survived the changing

A typical *beche de mer* curing shed. The sea slugs were laid out on the battens above and fires were lit underneath.

times as it had survived the early European interest in sandal-wood which was found on the south-west end of Vanua Levu. By 1804 the trade was well on the way with three ships taking cargoes. The profits were phenomenal, as was the opportunity for the Fijians to obtain guns by which they could have extended their influence. Within ten years the trade was largely finished and the chiefdoms which had prospered had once again sunk to anonymity, whilst Bau, which had no such advantage, continued to expand its power. Though Bau reaped none of the benefits of the lucrative sandalwood trade, it obtained most from what was to follow — the recovery of the seaslug *bech de mer*. Numerous ships called to collect cargoes and took these to Manilla. The profits were not as great as in the sandalwood trade, the cargoes requiring a great deal of time and effort to be obtained and cured. The ships had to move about the various reefs where they were in constant danger of shipwreck and attack. Among the many who

Hazards in Fiji were not confined to treacherous reefs and hungry cannibals. Hurricanes could come with sudden fury during the summer months, causing havoc and destruction as this picture shows of Levuka. (Caines Jannif archives photo.)

came to Fiji was David Whippy. He arrived on his brother's ship in the 1820s, left the ship and settled in the islands, eventually coming to play a prominent role in its politics and founding a shipyard which is still run by his descendants to this day. He was highly regarded by both Fijians and Europeans and was appointed vice-consul for the United States.

Whippy came from New Hampshire, but there were beachcombers and settlers from many parts of the globe. Most appear to have come from Great Britain. There were several negroes and an American Indian who owned an island and ran a prosperous business on Kadavu. Initially these men had acted as mercenaries, armourers and mechanics and interpreters to visiting ships.

In the 1830s, by the time the trade for seaslugs was well under way, a colony of these men had established itself at Levuka, in Ovalua. It was conveniently close to Bau as well as the islands of Lau, Taveuni and Vanua Levu. The port had the advantage of laying to the right quarter for the arrival and departure of sailing ships. Though the profit was not as great as it had been for sandalwood, it was still attractive enough for ship owners to take the risk and, of the recorded transactions, one ship got a cargo of 840 picules (approximately 60 kg per picule) at a cost of $1,200 which returned $12,000 in Manilla.

The Europeans had been happy to enjoy Bau's protection but were not so happy when Cakobau had their town burnt in revenge

138

for their refusal to help him in his war with Somosomo in 1841. They were not happy to pay tribute to Bau for seaslugs and generally began to resent the proud and overbearing nature of Cakobau and the havoc he was causing in Fiji. There was no part of eastern Fiji, whether the Lau Islands, Taveuni or Vanua Levu that did not see Bauan war parties. They raided, levied, demanded feasts and entertainment and pillaged and murdered. In 1843 there were seven wars in progress.

The triumphant progress which Cakobau launched to consolidate Bau's pre-eminence and his own ambition to claim the title of Tui Viti (King of Fiji) was not to proceed smoothly. European and Tongan ambitions would see to that, until finally, he would humbly cede his power with that of the other principal chiefs to Britain so that it would not be wrested from him by adventurers and those he described as the "cormorants on the beach". But all that was well in the future. Cakobau was young and powerful. He enjoyed what he called the "customs of the land" and not necessarily just because such customs justified his position and his tyrannical behaviour. Christianity, which was making inroads among his people, was not fun. It was against war, cannibalism, intrigue and lies, against the strangling of widows and against polygamy. The conversion of Namosimalua and his nephew, Varani, the two powerful men of Viwa, posed additional problems.

These men were the arm of Bau and none had a more terrible reputation or were feared as much. Namosimalua's conversion would seem to have been based more on politics than faith. He and Varani had seized the French ship, the l'Aimable Josephine, and killed the captain and most of the crew. Namosimalua saw the houses and plantations of View destroyed in a reprisal and also believed that he was in further danger from visiting French warships. His acceptance of Christianity may have been prompted by his belief that as a Christian he would not be punished.

Varani was different. He was regarded as one of the outstanding men of his time, both as a heathen and later as a Christian. He was Cakobau's closest friend and ally and a fearless, ruthless warrior who had blazed a trail of destruction from one end of Fiji to the other. His acceptance of the lotu was disastrous for Cakobau because it was sincere and because Varani intended to live by his faith. In his cannibal days Varani (the name is the Fijian transliteration of France) was a master of intrigue and treachery. The best example of his ability in this respect was the entrapment of the warriors of Namena. The incident occurred during the war with Somosomo in 1841 when the people of Verata went to the aid of Somosomo. Varani pretended rebellion against Cakobau and lured some one hundred Namena men to Viwa to help defend it. Cakobau landed and during his attack the hapless victims were killed, butchered and eaten. Such a man was difficult to replace. Namosimalua, his uncle, was the high chief of the Ra coast where he was able to call on some of Bau's best warriors and his reluctance to fight, because of his conversion, was equally serious.

In 1844 Cakobau banished the white traders from Levuka and it was not until 1849 that they were able to return. In that same year, the American Consul, John Brown Williams, also added to Cakobau's troubles. Williams was celebrating the fourth of July when salvos fired from muskets and cannon were adding much to the festivities. One of the cannons exploded and accidentally set fire to the house which Williams had built on Nukulau Island near the mouth of the Rewa River. The many people who were present took the opportunity to seize what they could and make off with it. Williams made up a bill and presented this to a visiting American warship. He claimed that $5,001.38 in goods had been stolen. Eventually this claim, as well as many others, was to come to roost at Cakobau's door and his excuse that he had not been responsible was not accepted. If he was the *Tui Viti*, he was responsible for his subjects' behaviour. By the time all the claims had been totalled they reached $44,000 and of this total, the original amount claimed by Williams had risen to $18,331. Cakobau was taken on board the American warship and, he claimed, made to sign an indemnity under threat of being transported to America. As he was already familiar with the fate of one of the Rewa chiefs who had been taken away in irons on board an American man-o-war never to be seen again, he had every reason to fear the same would happen to him.

It was the Tongan chief Maafu, however, who was to prove the most painful of Cakobau's many thorns. He was a prince of the royal blood and it was suggested that he be sent to take charge of the bands of Tongan warriors in Fiji by King George of Tonga as a precaution to remove a rival. He showed himself to have been one of the most able men of his generation and, had it not been for European intervention, would have brought most of Fiji under his control. His gains were made at the expense of Bau,

Enele Maafuotuitonga, known as Maafu, who very nearly came to rule Fiji.

first in Lakeba and Lau, later at Taveuni and Vanua Levu and then on Viti Levu itself. He set loose the Tongan mercenaries to carry out his will and masked this by pretending that he was acting on behalf of aggrieved and oppressed Christians and as a protector of Tongans. In this way he did what Bau had done before him and countless oppressors from generations past: those inviting his help would find themselves in the same position as did the christian chief on Vanua Balavu whom Maafu helped defeat his foes — instead of having gained a friend, the victorious chief had gained a master.

The Wesleyan Missionaries saw through his sham and when Maafu subdued Matuku, claiming he did so to protect Tongan Wesleyan teachers, he was expelled from membership of the Church; a fact Maafu chose to ignore as it was too convenient for his policy. Thus, by 1850 Cakobau had every reason to feel concerned and no doubt he would look back on the decade just passed with growing nostalgia.

Maafu himself posed as a man of law and order who had come to Fiji to curb his unruly countrymen. He was a sophisticated Tongan aristocrat, coming as a friend of King George and therefore a friend of Cakobau. He wore the mantle of protector of missionaries and patron of traders and settlers whom he encouraged in his expanding dominions. The Tongan chiefs Wainiqolo and Semisi Fifita he held as trumps in his hand, ready to play them

A typical Fijian bure with the people clearly Christians because of their dress, showing the type of modesty which pleased the Wesleyan missionaries. (Caines Jannif archives photo.)

wherever opportunity presented itself.

In the name of Christianity these two ravaged much of Fiji, passing over provinces like a swarm of locusts and leaving them

140

bare behind them. Maafu's talent and genius lay in his administration so that by 1855 he had acquired control over Northern Lau, Taveuni and Vanua Levu and united all northern and eastern Fiji in a well-governed confederacy. But his supreme ambition was to dispose of Cakobau and assume his mantle of *Tui Viti*, making Fiji part of a Tongan empire which would stretch as far west as the New Hebrides (Vanuatu) and Samoa to the north east. As Maafu's star rose that of Cakobau declined. It was one thing to claim to be the King of Fiji and quite another to cope with the problems of being regarded as one. The Europeans, in perceiving his loss of *mana*, were no longer so happy to pay him his dues. When Cakobau acquired two European schooners by undertaking to pay for these with *bech de mer*, the traders at Levuka did not hesitate to purchase these direct from those who had collected them for Cakobau, thus depriving him of his gain. In 1853 they ignored his authority altogether and took direct action. One of their cutters was taken by a town subject to Bau and Viwa and plundered and the crew taken ashore. When news reached Levuka an expedition was immediately fitted out and a request by the Tui Levuka to accompany it with some of his men was accepted. Unbeknown to the traders, Tui Levuka had a grudge against the people of Malaki. When the attack was made 14 people were killed and 13 taken prisoner, among them several women who were retained by the white men and kept at Ovalau. The seriousness of their situation dawned upon them. The Lovoni tribe, living in the mountains and valleys just behind the township were subject to Viwa and applied to Varani to avenge the insult. Varani had *lotued* and, as a Christian, he refused to allow the Lovoni to act. But, despite this restraint, somehow the township was set alight and the traders lost a great deal of property. Fearing worse things to come they joined the Tui Levuka and together bribed the Lovoni to rebel against Bau and Viwa. This rebellion was rightly regarded by Cakobau as of the gravest importance. The war with Rewa had lately been going against him and now the European traders had conspired with the mountaineers to blockade Bau from the sea and from visiting ships. In this extremity he turned for help to his old friend Varani of Viwa who volunteered to try and win back his rebellious subjects.

Varani took with him his two brothers and four other men. They landed at night and by the morning had reached the village. Naduva, one of two principal chiefs, received them and accepted their gifts of *tabua*. The other chief was at Levuka and when news reached him of Varani's arrival he immediately sent gifts to the interior and promised them his sister if they would kill Varani. One of the lesser chiefs, with a grudge against Varani, agreed to do the job and immediately set out. The next morning Varani, his two brothers and three of his party were shot and clubbed and some of them eaten. The bodies of Varani and his brothers were brought to Levuka where the murderers were amply rewarded for their deed. The loss of Varani, his close and trusted friend, was a severe blow to Cakobau, but worse was to follow. Ratu Kamisese Mara who had lately fled Bau was brought from Lakeba to tighten the noose around Bau. The Lovoni formed an alliance with Rewa and the traders of Levuka, the aim of which was the death of Cakobau. It was intended to install Mara and the Tui Levuka as the supreme chiefs, but they would rule at the wish of the Europeans. He was now blockaded from Ovalau and from a fort established at Kaba while many people, formerly his subjects, were now joining his enemies. At this decisive moment he received a letter from King George of Tonga urging Cakobau to *lotu*. After a few days he took the decisive step and on April 30, 1854, a service was held at Bau. Calvert describes the event thus:

"At nine o'clock the death-drum *rogorogoi valu* (reporter of war) was beaten. Ten days before, its sound had called the people together to a cannibal feast; now it gave the signal for assembling in the great Strangers' House for the worshipping of the true God. About three hundred people were in the building, before whom stood the Vunivalu, with his children and many wives and relatives. In front of him was his priest, an old man with grey hair and a long beard. All had assumed the more ample *lotu* dress, and were well behaved and serious. . . . That was a day ever to be remembered as one of the most important in the annals of Fiji."

The profession of Christianity had no immediate benefit for Cakobau. His enemies were strengthened by his conversion and Qaraniqio elated as more flocked to his cause. Two plots were set at Bau to kill Cakobau but he survived these with the intervention of the missionaries and then, just as he seemed to fall, his most implacable enemy Qaraniqio fell ill with dysentery and died in 1855. At the time of death he was unconscious and unable to leave instructions for the continuation of the war. With his death, a great deal of urgency for the coming attack was diffused.

Cakobau took the opportunity to try and bring about peace but Mara continued to agitate for its continuance and, surrounded by Bauan rebels, warriors of Rewa and heathen chiefs, prepared a new assault.

At this decisive moment two thousand warriors under King George of Tonga and Maafu of Lakeba, arrived in 39 canoes. The purpose of the visit was to collect a gift which Cakobau had promised to King George. This was the magnificent canoe, the *Ra Marama*. The less obvious reason was Tongan political interest in Fiji. It would seem that the Tongans came to mediate but gave weight to their mediation with the presence of 2000 experience warriors. It would have been enough to bring about peace in which they could hold power and thus advance a step further the plan of Tongan domination of Fiji. The rebels of Kaba and their allies at Levuka saw the Tongans as adversaries and when one of the canoes diverted to Levuka to deliver letters to the French priests, being forwarded from the French Governor of Tahiti, the canoe came under fire as it approached the beach and the Tongan chief Tawake, a relative of King George, was shot dead. The Tui Levuka stopped the shooting and the Tongans got away in time to avoid a canoe with a force of Fijians under the command of Mara, which at that moment was entering the lagoon. Four days later the combined force of two thousand Tongans and one thousand Fijians moved to attack Kaba. The Fijians took their position on the landward side and the Tongans landed from the sea. The plan was to lay siege to the fortress and reduce it by starvation. As the Tongans cut down some tress with which to build a pallisade, the Fijians made a sortie and killed several Tongans and dragged their bodies into their fortress. The Tongans made an impulsive charge, passed over the barricades, gained the interior and fired the houses. The Fijians fell back to another position. This was the main fortification. As the Tongans continued their charge they came under heavy fire and a number fell dead and others were wounded. As they fell, the Fijians considered the battle won, but the Tongans knew nothing of such rules and continued their charge, breached the defences and routed the defenders. At this moment Cakobau's troops swept in from the opposite end and a fearful slaughter began. Though they had contributed little to the assault the Fijians began the massacre and before their frenzy could be curbed they had butchered 180 men, women and children. The Tongans, who had taken the brunt of the fire, lost 14 killed and twenty wounded. Of the two hundred prisoners, all were spared including Koroi Ravulo, a chief whom Cakobau wanted to execute. Mara was not among those taken, having escaped with some of his men during the battle. In the peace that followed, the missionaries saw their efforts rewarded. They had stood by Cakobau and when his battle was won, the gods of old were swept away and the people turned to *lotu*. The Tongans left on their return voyage, the King travelling on the *Ra Marama* with the fleet which included the schooner, *Cakobau*, bringing other lavish gifts, for they had in fact saved Cakobau's life and averted the destruction of Bau. Yet though they were sailing out of Fiji, the Tongans were leaving behind Maafu and his men whose prestige would now be greater than ever and whose arrogance could not be checked. Maafu now made his move: playing off one chief against another and posing as a deliverer while meaning to be an exploiter, he divided the Fijian forces and gained power at their expense.

OFFER OF CESSION

Cakobau found small satisfaction in the position to which King George of Tonga had restored him. He was haunted by fear of his Tongan deliverers and worried about the money being claimed by Williams and the other Americans. His debt he felt was most unjustly set against him, but he knew that it was also impossible for him to pay it even had he been willing to do so. In this state he turned to the British consul and proposed to cede Fiji to Britain. William Thomas Pritchard, the new consul, had only recently arrived in Fiji from Samoa and had no reason to doubt the claims that Cakobau made as to his status in Fiji. When Cakobau signed the deed of cession in October, 1858, he claimed to be the Chief of Bau and its dependencies, Vunivalu of the armies of Fiji, and Tui Viti; to having been formally recognised as such by Great Britain, Franch, and the United States; and to possess full and exclusive sovereignty and dominion throughout the group. In offering to cede Fiji to Britain, he stipulated that he should retain the title Tui Viti, that he should be the head of the Native Department under the Queen's representative, and that the Imperial Government should fully discharge the United States Government's claim for $45,000. In return for the outlay he offered not less than 200,000 acres of land. Pritchard sailed for England. He returned a year later to find Maafu in a dominant position and

A group of European planters from the 1870s.

ready to launch a final blow against Bau, to which at this stage he was still professing friendship. Cakobau appealed to Pritchard to restrain Maafu on the grounds that Fiji was already ceded to Britain. Maafu also approached Pritchard and explained how much better it would be for Fiji and the European powers if Cakobau, whom he called "that old savage", were overthrown.

Maafu promised that if he were to be master of Fiji he would not oppose annexation and would place himself under any representative of the Queen. Pritchard hesitated. He now knew that Cakobau did not occupy the paramount position which he claimed in the deed of cession and it was doubtful that he owned or controlled 200,000 acres of land which he offered in consideration of payment of the American claims. Pritchard decided to resolve the situation by calling all the important chiefs to a general meeting in Levuka and with a British man-o-war in the harbour to dampen the ardour of the hostile factions, persuaded Maafu to renounce all political claims on and in Fiji, and the lands conquered. He made Maafu sign a declaration to that effect.

He next prevailed on the chiefs to add their signatures to an agreement which ratified and renewed Cakobau's offer of cession and added clauses regulating the conduct of the Fijians with Europeans. In their enthusiasm the chiefs asked him to head a native government and Pritchard accepted. His extra-consular activity, however, was not well received in London where also at the end of that year, a Colonel W. T. Smythe, R.A. was instructed to proceed and report on whether Cakobau's offer should be accepted. As soon as the possibility of cession became known, more settlers began arriving. There were obvious benefits to be gained if Britain were to accept cession. But Smythe advised against it and once again the country was thrown into unrest. The result of the uncertainty as to the future encouraged Maafu, who despite signing agreements and formal documents not to interfere in Fiji, continued to do so with the intention of becoming master of Bau and having Cakobau "cook for me". He claimed $60,000 for the Tongan services at the battle of Kaba and entered into a secret alliance with Rewa against Bau. But it was not all plain sailing. In 1861 the French corvette *Cornelie* arrived in Levuka and after hearing a complaint from the French Catholic mission about Tongan atrocities against Catholics in the Yasawa Islands conducted an inquiry which lead to the conviction of Maafu's lieutenant Semisi Fifita who was sentenced to hard labour in the French penal settlement of New Caledonia, from where nothing more was heard of him in Fiji. Cakobau and Maafu were present at the trial and the lesson was not lost on them — especially Maafu, who abandoned for a few months his plans against Bau. Early the next year he renewed his attempt with greater determination and once again, when war between Bau and Maafu seemed imminent, Pritchard took decisive action. He sailed to Tonga to make a direct appeal to King George only to find Maafu already there waiting to receive him. The complicity of the King in Maafu's designs was now made obvious and Pritchard played his trump card again: Smythe had not yet reported against the acceptance of cession. King George was persuaded to sign an agreement to do nothing until this question was resolved.

The European community in Levuka, now considerably swelled by men of substance and capital, had ideas of its own. They wanted land and cheap labour and they wanted these things under a British administration. Some of the transactions were so patently unfair that Pritchard intervened on behalf of the Fijians and had the land returned to them. His actions increased opposition to him. In 1862 the Imperial Government advised the chiefs of Fiji that their offer of cession could not be accepted. The Wesleyan Missionaries also turned on Pritchard, convinced that he was opposed to them and their work and added their considerable weight to a move to have him removed. In 1863 he was removed from office and though he hastened to London to defend himself he was not able to clear his name. In retrospect, he is seen as a man ahead of his time who did all he could to introduce law and order into a chaotic situation. His reward was a bitter failure and personal tragedy. He and his wife left Fiji by separate passage only to learn on reaching Tonga that his sister and his two young daughters had been lost at sea in a hurricane while on the way to Samoa. He left England for Mexico and later set out overland for California. Nothing more was heard of him and it was supposed that he had been captured and killed by Red Indians.

Those of the new settlers who had rushed to Fiji in anticipation of its annexation by Britain were looking forward to successful investment in Fiji. Such an investment depended on the availability of land and labour — at cheap prices. Cotton had been found to thrive in Fiji. The Civil War in the United States had made availability extremely scarce and gave an opportunity to growers in Fiji to reap a handsome profit. In 1864 cotton exports earned some $7000 and in 1866, $50,000. The Fijians, however, did not understand that land sold to Europeans was alienated forever and the Europeans failed to appreciate that it was impossible to buy land outright and often chose to ignore many other complications such as land which was sold by chiefs who had no authority to do so. Even when such land was sold within the territories claimed by Cakobau, he could not protect the settlers from robbery and violence. This was not universally so, for in Lau Maafu knew how to keep settlers from being molested. In 1865 Maafu formed his Lau Confederation which included the chiefs of Lau, Cakaudrove (Taveuni and eastern Vanua

Levu) and Bua, also in Vanua Levu. In the same year Bau formed a confederacy of its own. Two years later Cakobau had a constitution drawn up and European residents came to Bau to discuss it. After deliberations extending over two days, the constitution was accepted for a three-year period and it was agreed that Cakobau's status as King of Fiji would be formally acknowledged with a coronation. The ceremony took place at Bau and all went well until the moment of crowning when the King took the crown. This was a contrivance made by a Levuka carpenter at a cost of $4.50. As Cakobau placed it on his head a titter ran through some of the guests who saw the absurdity of the situation. Cakobau's natural dignity and grace averted what could have been unrestrained laughter. He was now installed as Tui Viti, the King of Fiji, but once again this step was only a prelude to the problems which would follow. In the interior, where the *Kei Colo* (the people from the bush), acknowledged no power but that of their own chiefs, the Wesleyan missionary, Thomas Baker, was killed and eaten at a village on the headwaters of the Sigatoka River. The place where he fell is marked by a small pile of stones, for those curious enough to make the trek, but his murder only served to embarrass Cakobau and show how ineffectual his authority really was. He could neither prevent the murder nor take immediate steps to punish the culprits. Nor was Cakobau's assumption of power recognised by the British consul who warned the settlers, most of whom were British, that if they placed themselves under the King's authority they would prejudice their right to protection from the British Government. They refused to pay the pol tax, leaving the Government without funds. That same year, soon after his coronation, an American warship arrived to demand settlement of his debt and, as he could not pay it, took a lien on some of his best islands as security for the debt. No sooner had the Americans left than the British arrived to press Cakobau to avenge the murder of Baker, but it was not until the following year that he acted, mounting a two-pronged assault to the heart of the interior. He took charge of one column himself and moved from the north, while another, led by his two sons entered from the south. In both cases the expeditions were disastrous. Cakobau fell into an ambush and lost 13 chiefs, while his sons lost 61 men killed.

The growing European presence had other unfortunate effects. As Fijian labourers were not always available for the plantations nor always willing even when available, the planters looked for other sources of labour. This eventually led to the notorious practice of "blackbirding" when ships of pirates scoured the islands of the South Pacific in search of human cargoes. The crews were paid head money and thus had the incentive to get results while the owners could get up to $30 per man — a vast amount in those days. The trade was so lucrative that recruiting ships used any means to get people aboard. They were coaxed, bought, kidnapped — often with the connivance of chiefs or enemies. It was one thing for the British Government to be aware of the trade, but another to stop it. There was no law to enforce as the British Government had failed to draw up the necessary legislation. In 1871 an event so gruesome took place that the necessary law was enacted.

The brig *Carl* had sailed out of Melbourne on a recruiting mission and had kidnapped a cargo of about 80 men by upsetting canoes or by dropping pig iron through them. The men were locked away in the hold but, as they were not of the same tribe, fighting broke out and turned into a riot. The crew panicked and began shooting into the hold through the bulkhead for eight hours. At daylight when the hatches were opened only five men came out; 25 were wounded and 50 dead. The dead and the wounded were thrown overboard and the ship cleaned and whitewashed to remove evidence. But at Levuka a part-owner of the ship who had been on board during the massacre, confessed to the consul. The master and one other were arrested, found guilty and sentenced to death. The part-owner, Murray, who had turned Queen's evidence, went free.

Abuse of indentured labourers was not confined to the way they were recruited. There were plantation owners who had scant regard for the rights of their workers and in many cases treated such labour as slave labour.

In 1869 the cotton boom went bust, adding to the problems of the settlers and merchants, in what were at best lawless and confused conditions. Several attempts were made to establish a government, or to at least find a formula on which one could be based but it was not until 1871 that the means were found. The Lovoni tribe, which had always menaced the Europeans at Levuka and which had been responsible for the death of Varani, refused to pay a tax to Cakobau. They followed this act of defiance by killing a chief and eating his body and by destroying a village and killing a further ten people. Cakobau arrived with a war fleet and lay siege to the Lovoni for two months. As his soldiers invested the fortress, Cakobau was scheming with the merchants of Levuka. With their willing help and his connivance, on June 5, 1871 Cakobau was proclaimed King of Fiji and those who had schemed with him were rewarded with ministerial title. Later in the month the Lovoni surrendered and were made to crawl on hands and knees before their conquerors, offering baskets of earth in deference to Fijian custom. But what followed rankles to this day: Cakobau had the whole tribe — men, women and children — marched into Levuka where it was broken up and sentenced to transportation as labour on European plantations. Cakobau took their lands and mortgaged these to Europeans who advanced money to his government. Planters paid $6 a head for the labourers and agreed to a yearly rental of the same amount. From the sale of the people he got more than $2000 which he used to launch his government and from the hire of their labour he received the money each year to keep his government afloat. While those who had conspired with Cakobau were happy at the turn of events, there were many others who were opposed to him and his ministers, both for personal reasons and because they had been given no voice in the matter. The new government was considerably bolstered when Maafu took the oath of allegiance in return for being made the Lieutenant-Governor of Lau, given the rank of Viceroy and a fixed income. He was also given clear title to the islands of Moala, Matuku and Totoya. Eventually all the other chiefs followed suit and it appeared as if the Government might succeed. But this was not to be. The Europeans who opposed it received support from the British consul who refused to act in support of Cakobau and intervene in matters where, if he had done so, the government would have received the status of legitimacy which was necessary for its successful continuation. The whites who opposed Cakobau formed themselves into the Ku-Klux-Klan and later adopted the title of the British Subjects' Mutual Protection Society and Volunteer Corps in an effort to gain support from the more responsible men in Levuka. The crisis came when a planter, who was alleged to have shot a Fijian chief, arrived in Levuka. A warrant had been issued for his arrest, yet he came openly to town and waited to see what the Government would do. The Volunteer Corps was called out and marched to the hotel where the planter was lodged. The 30 riflemen marched

Not all plantation owners treated their "blackbirded" labour badly as this picture would tend to prove. The white *turaga* poses with his shotgun, while his Solomon Islands labourers hold their traditional weapons.

about with fixed bayonets but, after parading, dispersed. March, the British consul, refused to intervene in support of the government or even to see its ministers. As matters came to a head,

A large outrigger canoe photographed at Bau post-cession. It is small in comparison to the great war canoes used by Cakobau. Some of these exceeded 100 feet and carried more than 250 warriors. The canoes were taken apart and the pieces buried in a swamp on Cakobau's death.

Cakobau addressed a meeting in Levuka and said: "We Fijians understand revenge, and the law of the club. You white people said such things were cruel and savage. You wanted civilization, and you brought us laws. Now there are divisions among you, and an appeal to force. If you resist the law and force us to settle matters in our old way, there will be a war of races. I appeal to you to support law and order."

The situation was relieved when one of Cakobau's European ministers, who had been largely responsible for the immediate disaffection of many of the whites through his arrogant and overbearing manner, resigned. Cakobau then sent for John Bates Thurston, a planter at Taveuni and a man who was to play a critical role in Fiji's future. He was an outstanding man who had served for two years as the British acting consul from 1867 and had won the support of all factions for his able and intelligent use of office. Thurston declined to join Cakobau's government, but the King determined to have his man and sent three successive envoys, in three ships, to persuade the reluctant would-be minister. When Thurston still refused, a large ship was chartered and a deputation embarked to convince him to join. Thurston agreed.

He arrived in Levuka to find a chaotic situation. Those who had opposed the government grew more defiant, while those who supported it formed themselves into a Mutual Defence Corps. But the real problem continued to be the British consul, March, who persisted in his defiance and non-recognition of the Government and it was now seen that he was the real (if unacknowledged) leader of the rebellious faction. The next crisis occurred when two members of the British Subjects' Mutual Protection Society committed an assault in Levuka and were arrested. The rebels had staged the scene for the benefit of a visiting British warship, intending to release the prisoners to show that the Cakobau government was a farce. Thurston had other ideas. He mustered the volunteers and police, numbering some 200 men, and ordered them to load their rifles with ball and cartridge, to arrest any malcontent found armed or on resistance to shoot him and to shoot down any persons attempting to break gaol. The Government force had two field pieces and ample ammunition. The Ku-Klux-Klan fell back on their stronghold which they had fortified and were there surrounded. The Captain of the British warship intervened and advised the rebels that British subjects domiciled in foreign countries were subject to the laws of those countries. This was a blow from which they never recovered. Though the government had won this round and showed that it was capable of maintaining law and order, its ultimate downfall would be its growing indebtedness. Once again there was talk of cession to Britain as a possible solution to some of the problems. It was certainly seen as an answer by the growing European presence.

A new outrage by the hill people who massacred a settler family on the banks of the Ba River led to another confrontation between Government forces and those who opposed Cakobau. Part of the old brigade who had formed the British Subjects' Mutual Protection Society arrived on the scene a day ahead of the government force and organised the local settlers into a punitive force whose first objective was to settle the matter on their own account. To do so they first had to deal with the government troops. The officer in charge of the government force retired with his troops in order to avoid a pitched battle. The matter was resolved (once again) on the deck of a British man-o-war when an agreement was signed and the ringleaders of the revolt were taken under arrest and eventually deported from Fiji. A campaign against the hill people followed which resulted in a victory of the government forces. A thousand prisoners were taken and many of them sentenced to penal servitude from three to seven years and offered to planters on the same basis as had the Lovoni two years previously. But the scheme was spoiled by Commodore Goodenough who arrived at Levuka while the sale was in progress and warned British subjects to have nothing to do with it so that few planters were willing to hire the prisoners.

It became more and more obvious, however, that the disaffected whites in Levuka wanted a government dominated by Europeans and for the benefit of Europeans. This was clearly seen by Thurston who opposed them in every way, especially when they tried to prevent the Fijians having the vote, and a section was already acting as if the country was theirs. In 1874 a commission arrived to inquire into the question of another offer of cession. Finally in March Cakobau, after several changes of heart, agreed to cede the islands and an interim government was established until the offer could be confirmed. With Thurston's advice, Cakobau attached a number of conditions and these included his retention of the title Tui Viti, the granting of pensions and perquisites to him and his sons and of positions and salaries to the principal chiefs, the confirmation of charters already granted to banking and land companies, the retention of existing rights by the Fijian people, and the recognition of the ruling chiefs as owners of the tribal lands and as guardians of their people's rights and interests. In September Sir Hercules Robinson arrived in Levuka in H.M.S. *Pearl* and advised Cakobau that the offer of cession would be accepted, but not with the conditions attached to it and Cakobau agreed. For two days the King and chiefs discussed the matter, approved a draft of the

Some members of the 'European community parade before the flagstaff at Levuka.

deed of cession and Cakobau, with four of the ruling chiefs then present, signed. Cakobau then boarded the *Pearl* to gather the signatures of Maafu, Tui Cakau and the chiefs of Vanua Levu. On October 10, 1874, a formal ceremony was held at Levuka where the King presented his old war club to Sir Hercules as a gift to Her Majesty the Queen of Great Britain. Thurston, speaking on behalf of Cakobau, said: "The King gives Her Majesty his old and favourite war club, the former, and until lately the only known, law of Fiji. In abandoning club law, and adopting the forms and principles of civilised societies, he laid by his old weapon and covered it with emblems of peace. Many of his people — whole tribes — died and passed away under the old law; but hundreds of thousands still survive to enjoy the newer and better state of things. The King adds only a few words. With this emblem of the past he send his love to Her Majesty, saying that he fully confides in her and her children, who, succeeding her, shall become Kings of Fiji, to exercise a watchful control over the welfare of his children and people, who having survived the barbaric law and age, are now submitting themselves under Her Majesty's rule to civilization.

The club was returned to Fiji in 1932 to become the mace of the Legislative Council and is now used in the House of Representatives.

The deed was signed by Cakobau, Maafu, Tui Cakau, Ratu Epeli, Tui Bua, Savenaca, Esekele, Tui Dreketi, Ritova, Katonivere, Ratu Kini, Matanitobua and Nacagilevu. Eventually the signatures of other important chiefs were added.

The most significant events to follow cession were the appointment of Thurston as Colonial Secretary, the appointment of Arthur Hamilton Gordon as the Governor and in 1879 the recruitment of indentured labour from India. Thurston had already shown himself to be a staunch friend of the Fijians and it was largely through him that in 1880 native lands were made inalienable and remain so to this day. Only 17% was recognised as having been fairly purchased prior to cession, but this included crown land as well. In 1881 the Colonial Sugar Refining Company of Australia began operations in Fiji. It was Thurston who had persuaded the company to set up in the new colony with the objective of having the company crush cane grown by Fijians both to meet their taxes and to earn a cash surplus. In the event, this proved impractical at the time but now, more than a hundred years later, increasing numbers of Fijians are doing just that. Thurston and Gordon were the right combination at the right time as far as the Fijians were concerned and the situation which had developed in other colonies never developed in Fiji. The Fijians kept their land and kept their status so that ninety-six years after cession, in 1970, they successfully took over the administration of their country.

The transition from Fijian custom to colonial administration was not without its problems. There was alarm over the growing strength of a new cult being espoused by a Ra prophet until he was seized and exiled first to Lau and later to Rotuma. The Tuka cult was against the new order and could not be allowed to exist.

A young Indian girl, richly attired as if for a wedding, in a solemn pose. Few women were brought during the early years of the indenture system, leading to bitter loneliness for the men. (Caines Jannif archives photo.)

It was also with alarm that the Fijians viewed the growing presence of Indian indentured labour, for this was yet another element being introduced which was once again different from

150

Armed native constabulary two years after cession, parade for inspection at Nasova, Levuka, in 1876.

what had gone previously. Today, the descendents of those humble labourers number more than half the population. They still comprise the heart of the sugar growing industry but they are also the mainstay of Fiji's professional, business and entrepreneurial class. The Indians came on five-year contracts and those early years when the first shiploads arrived in Fiji were later described as hell. Many were to return to India, but many more chose to remain in Fiji and go into business on their own account if at all possible. Their growing presence and success alarmed the Fijians who asked the administration what the future would be for those who decided to settle in Fiji and Thurston answered that they were British subjects and could settle in Fiji if they wished.

Whilst the Fijians viewed the growing Indian presence with anxiety the white community, which had been so happy with British annexation, were less happy at the Gordon-Thurston administration. They wanted cheap land and cheap labour and, as they could not quite get either, many of them went bankrupt. Thurston succeeded Gordon as Governor and continued his policy of protecting and encouraging Fijian autonomies in opposition to those who urged the Colonial Office to bring the administration in Fiji in line with that of other colonies. But with Thurston's death in the 1890s and the passing of many Europeans and Fijians who had supported Thurston and his vision of Fiji, the balance tilted in favour of the white minority which was still clamouring for cheap land. They wanted clause 4 of the Deed of Cession applied and this read: "That the absolute proprietorship of all lands not shown to be now alienated so as to have become bona fide the property of Europeans or other foreigners or not now in actual use or occupation of some Chief or tribe or not actually required for the probable future support and maintenance of some chief or tribe shall be and is hereby declared to be vested in Her said Majesty her heirs and successors." In 1908 this was applied and some 104,412 acres of Fijian land was sold before Sir Arthur Gordon, now a Member of the House of Lords as Lord Stanmore, reminded the Colonial Office that Fijian land was inalienable. And despite the best efforts of the white population in Fiji and their supporters in the Colonial Office, it remained inalienable. And so, 111 years after the Deed of Cession was signed 83% of the land remains in the hands of the Fijians, even though, as Ron Crocombe of the University of the South Pacific has pointed out, much of the best of it is on long-term leases to people other than Fijian.

The new century brought with it many new problems. Indian indentured labour was still coming in and would not cease until two years after the start of the Great War in 1914. The war also brought to prominence Ratu Lala Sukuna, who was to become Fiji's outstanding statesman. Ratu Sukuna was at Oxford when war broke out but his offer to join the British forces was declined on the basis of colour. The French accepted him with open arms, however, and he went off to the front where in 1915 he was wounded while charging with his unit against the German line. He had been sent to Oxford by the Fijian people, who had realised they would need leaders able to cope with their rapidly changing world. Ratu Sukuna, later Sir Lala Sukuna, with his experience at Oxford and the Great War, returned to Fiji to urge his countrymen to embrace progress and the new ways if it would lead to their economic advancement, but there were not enough Fijian people with the right qualifications to compete successfully against the growing European commercial interests or to succeed against Indian and Chinese traders. Despite the best intentions of Thurston and his vision of Fiji as a colony managed for the benefit of Fijians and not for the benefit of a tiny European minority, in the end Fiji became an exclusive European club dominated by the Colonial Sugar Refining Company and the giant firms of Carpenters, Morris Headstrom and Burns Philp. Whilst the Indians began to view this club with increasing annoyance and resentfulness, the Fijians for their part began to view the growing Indian presence with alarm. So much so that in 1933 the Council of Chiefs resolved that: Fiji, having been ceded to her Majesty the Queen of Great Britain and Ireland, Her Heirs and Successors, the immigrant Indian population should neither directly nor indirectly have any part in the control or direction of matters affecting the control of the Fijian race.

The Indians wanted franchise. They wanted democracy. They wanted one vote for one man, but this was not what all of them wanted for there were minorities within the Indian community and this was certainly not what the Fijians wanted. The European merchant princes, the colonial civil servants on their tour of duty, secure with privilege and pomp and living in grandeur behind Government House, also wanted things to stay pretty much as they were: the Indians in their segregated compartment, the Fijians in their *koro* and the other minorities, such as part-Europeans and the Chinese, in their proper place.

But nothing stays the same. World War II changed the status quo much more quickly than anyone could have foreseen. Fijian troops went off to battle against the Japanese in the Solomon Islands; a large American garrison and depot was established at Lautoka. New winds with new ideas began to blow. They blew hardest for the Indian community which saw the colonial system as discriminatory and repressive and the huge Colonial Sugar Refining Company as a paternalistic monopoly making excessive profits at their expense. But Indian resolve to fight for equality socially and politically and for what they saw as a better share of profit from growing cane, was not united. It was at this

A race of Fijian outrigger canoes on Suva Harbour in the 1920s.

time that the charismatic and fiery A. D. Patel angered a large number of Indian farmers by forming a union in opposition to the Kisan Sangh, the first farmers' union in Fiji. Patel formed the rival cane farmers' union, the Akhil Fiji Krishnik Maha Sangh. In 1943 the union called its farmers on strike and cane was either burnt as it stood, or allowed to rot on the fields. The strike was

aimed at getting farmers a larger slice of the cake, but it was yet another expression of Indian dissatisfaction with the colonial system and their place in it.

The Indian community was also divided on what to do about war. While the Fijians went off to fight, the Indians were in two minds: some joined the war effort by enlisting in the Labour

Temple of Komai Natavasara, the great war god of Somosomo as it appeared in the late 1840s. (From *Fiji and the Fijians*, Vol 1, 1858).

Corps, while others would have nothing to with it. Understandably this led to bitter resentfulness about the Fijians, and especially Ratu Sukuna who was to assume such an important role in Fiji's post-war affairs.

In 1946 the Indian population became greater than the Fijian, adding yet more anxiety to the Fijian people that somehow they were being left behind. The Indians, for their part, saw things quite differently: they were the ones who were getting no benefit from the country to which they had contributed so much.

Ratu Sir Lala Sukuna died in 1958. The next year Suva streets erupted into riots where much of the dissatisfaction felt by both Fijians and Indians was expressed in violence. The cause of the riots was a strike by the General Workers' Union seeking better wages for its members.

In 1960 the cane growers went on strike. But Fiji was entering the jet age, the new airstrip having been completed at Nadi, and events were to take place at a much faster rate. The new decade brought with it a new interest in Fiji's political future and saw the emergence of Ratu Kamisese Mara, who has continued to dominate the political stage since then. He became Leader of Government Business and then in 1970 took Fiji to independence and nationhood, and became the country's first Prime Minister of a multi-racial party, the Alliance. He is the Prime Minister today, having held power continuously except during the election of 1977 which he lost. This was due to internal divisions within the Fijian community and not to loss of Mara's popularity. The problem arose when a former member of the Alliance, Sakiasi Butadroka formed the Fijian Nationalist Party and entered the election on the manifesto that all Indians and other foreigners should be thrown out of Fiji.

Butadroka had already made his intention clear in 1975 when, as a Member of Parliament, he had moved a motion in the House for the expulsion of the Indian community from Fiji. The motion was lost. But Butadroka's sentiment was shared by the Fijians who gave him enough votes to cost Mara the election. The National Federation party won with a majority of two but failed to take office, in yet another classic demonstration of the internal divisions which are a fact of life in Fiji. Butadroka cost Mara the election, a faction opposed to S. M. Koya, the Prime Minister elect, cost him the office.

When, after four days Koya failed to form a Government, the Governor-General called on Mara, now Ratu Sir Kamisese, to form an administration. As soon as he did so, senior members went out to the provinces to mend fences and to explain why Butadroka's party and its policy had very nearly the opposite effect to what they sought: giving the country an Indian administration. The Prime Minister called an election later that year and won. The Federation Party discarded Koya in the meantime and mended its won fences so that it went into the 1982 election confident of victory, but the election was marred by acrimony and the Federation Party lost. Butadroka, restrained by a Public Order Act faded from the political stage and now raises chickens and dalo on his property near Suva.

Many of the anxieties and tensions which had marked Fiji as an emerging nation remain. Many others, such as the Colonial Sugar Refining Company, which was seen as an oppressive monopoly, are gone. The company sold its interest to the Fiji Government and now, in retrospect, it is remembered fondly. Other issues, such as the availability of land for the growing population — both Indian and Fijian — will always remain because there is not enough to go round. The Indians, most of whom are tenant farmers, want continuity of leases whilst Fijians, who are increasingly turning to cane farming, want some of their land back as well as access to leases.

No one talks much these days of one man and one vote. The Fijians want to be able to "catch up" to the others academically and economically. There is a commitment to development and diversification of the economy. Fiji made a decision to develop tourism in the 1960s and the growth in this industry has been spectacular. Sugar, despite fluctuations in price, continues a major industry. Future prospects include a large timber industry based on extensive plantings of Caribbean pine, a fishing industry which already services a cannery at Levuka and some processing industries. It is a country which has come to terms with its problems whilst looking forward to a brighter future.

FACTS ABOUT FIJI

The total land area of Fiji is 18,333 square kilometres, spread over 332 islands covering thousands of square kilometres of ocean. The largest island is Viti Levu which has 10,429 square kilometres of land, Vanua Levu has 5,556, Taveuni 470, Kadavu 411, Gau 140, Koro 104, Ovalau 101, Rabi 69, Rotuma 47 and Beqa 36. The islands lie between 15 degrees of latitude south of the equator and 22 degrees south. The 180th degree of longitude, which marks the international dateline, passes through the group.

Since becoming an independent nation in 1970 after 96 years of British Colonial rule, Fiji has been a member of the Commonwealth with close ties to Britain. Fiji recognises Queen Elizabeth II as the Queen of Fiji, whose representative is the Governor-General. The current office holder is Ratu Sir Penaia Ganilau.

The Legislative Assembly consists of two chambers: a House of Representatives elected on a preferential communal basis and a

Senate of appointed members. The House of Representatives has 52 elected members and the Senate has 22 appointed members. The Governor-General appoints members of the Senate on nomination by the Great Council of Chiefs (eight seats), the Prime Minister (seven), the Leader of the Opposition (six) and the Council of Rotuma (one). The current Parliament was elected in the fourth general election since independence. The election took place in 1982. The ruling Alliance Party won 28 seats. The National Federation Party 22 and the Western United Front 2. The Federation Party and the Western United Front have formed a coalition party.

The Fijian electoral system is based on a communal grouping of the major ethnic blocks. It is established on universal suffrage for all citizens of 21 years of age and over who register on three separate rolls — Fijian, Indian or General as well as on an additional roll, the National Roll. Parliament consists of 22 Fijian seats, 22 Indian seats and 8 General Elector seats. For the Fijians and Indians, 12 are elected by voters on the Communal Roll and 10 by voters on the National Roll. For General Elector representatives, three are elected by voters on the Communal Roll and five by voters on the National Roll. A voter casts a vote for his communal representative and votes for each of the three national representatives in whose constituency he resides. Elections are held every five years except when Parliament is dissolved earlier either by choice of the Prime Minister or by the Governor-General following a constitutional crisis.

The economy of Fiji is dependent on the growing of cane for the purpose of sugar manufacture for export. The cane is grown mainly on small holdings and crushed by the Government-owned Fiji Sugar Corporation in a number of mills located through the growing areas. The sugar is partly refined.

Tourism is now second to sugar as a major earning of hard currency and there are indications that it may become the principal industry in the near future. More than 200,000 visitors came in 1984 and the popularity of Fiji is growing rapidly as a holiday destination. It attracts an increasing stream of visitors from Australia, New Zealand, the United States, Canada, Japan and South East Asia.

Other major exports are gold, copra, fish, coconut products and coconut oil, timber, ginger and certain processed consumer goods. The Government has followed several development plans

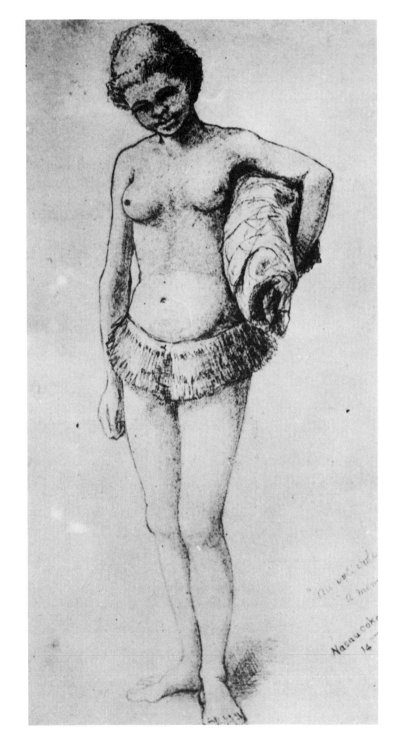

with the principal aim of making Fiji more self-sufficient through all sectors.

Fiji is the cross-roads of the South Seas and as such, is a natural destination for a number of international airlines linking the northern hemisphere with Australia and New Zealand. The country also has its own international airline, Air Pacific, which also runs a domestic service. Suva, Lautoka and Levuka are the ports of entry.

There are more than 3000 kilometres of road with the busiest section being the all-weather sealed highway between Lautoka and Suva, known as the Queen's Road. Work has begun on improvements to the road around east Viti Levu which is known as the King's Road.

CLIMATE

Fiji enjoys a tropical maritime climate without extremes of heat or cold. This is attractive to visitors from the colder climates. The Fijian winter is warm and dry and made fresh with the south-east trade winds. It is appreciated by New Zealanders and South Australians.

The summer contrasts with the Northern Hemisphere's winter and is equally attractive. The islands, however, lie in the area occasionally traversed by tropical cyclones during the summer period between November and April. Maximum temperatures during the summer are usually about 30 degrees celsius and approximately 28 degrees during the winter. Most rainfall is confined to the windward side which faces the south east trade winds. During the summer, the western side also enjoys adequate rainfall.

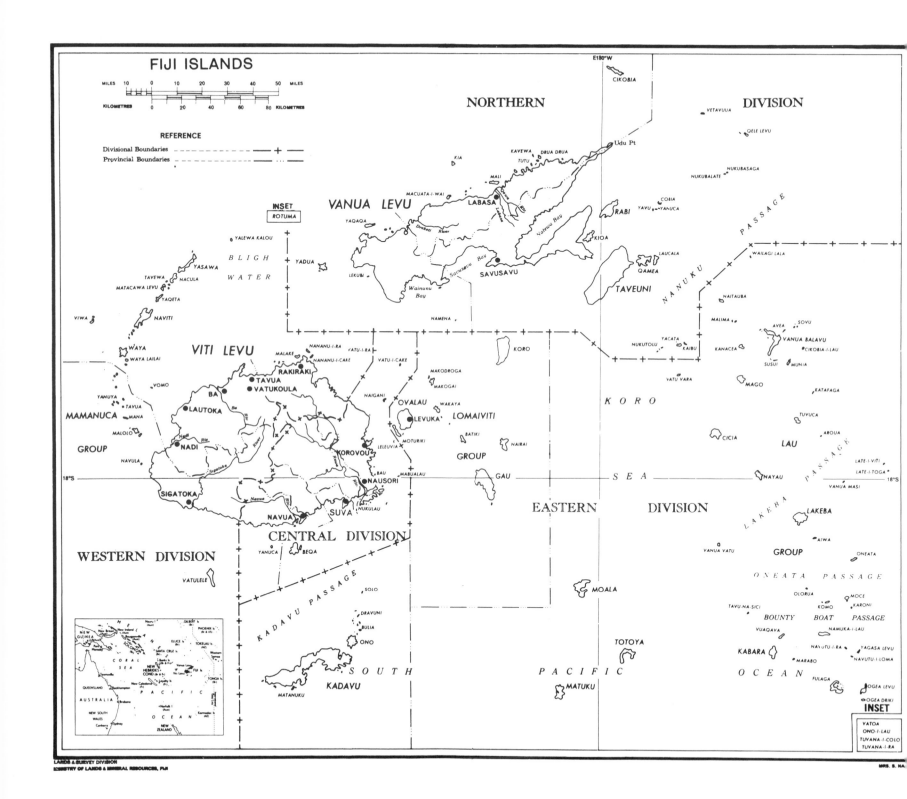

FIJI ISLANDS

MILES 10   0   10   20   30   40   50   MILES

KILOMETRES   0   20   40   60   80   KILOMETRES

REFERENCE

Divisional Boundaries — — — — +

Provincial Boundaries — — — —

INSET
ROTUMA

NORTHERN   **DIVISION**

CIKOBIA

VETAVUUA

QELE LEVU

NUKUBASAGA

NUKUBALATE

VANUA LEVU

KIA   KAVEWA   DRUA DRUA   Udu Pt

MACUATA-I-WAI   MALI   TUTU

LABASA

COBIA

RABI   YAVU   YANUCA

KIOA

LAUCALA

QAMEA

TAVEUNI

YAQAQA

LEKUBI

Dreketi River

Savusavu Bay

SAVUSAVU

Wainunu Bay

NAMENA

NANUKU   PASSAGE

WAILAGI LALA

NAITAUBA

MALIMA

AVEA   SOVU

VANUA BALAVU

CIKOBIA-I-LAU

SUSUI   MUNIA

NUKUTOLU   YACATA

KAIBU   KANACEA

VATU VARA

MAGO

KATAFAGA

YALEWA KALOU

BLIGH

WATER

YADUA

YASAWA

TAVEWA   NACULA

MATACAWA LEVU

YAQETA

VIWA

NAVITI

WAYA

WAYA LAILAI

VITI LEVU

MALAKE

NANANU-I-RA   VATU-I-RA

NANANU-I-CAKE   VATU-I-CAKE

RAKIRAKI

TAVUA

VATUKOULA

BA

NAIGANI

MAKODROGA

MAKOGAI

MAKOGAI

OVALAU   WAKAYA

LEVUKA   LOMAIVITI

LAUTOKA

Ba River

MOTURIKI

BATIKI

NAIRAI

GROUP

KORO

KORO

YANUYA

TAVUA   MANA

MAMANUCA

MALOLO

GROUP

NAVULA

Nadi River

NADI

Sigatoka River

KOROVOU

BAU   MABUALAU

NAUSORI

LELEUVIA

GAU

SEA

LAU

CICIA

TUVUCA

AROUA

LATE-I-VITI

LATE-I-TOGA

VANUA MASI

18°S   NAYAU   18°S

SIGATOKA

Navua River

NAVUA   SUVA

NUKULAU

LAKEBA

AIWA

EASTERN   **DIVISION**

VANUA VATU

GROUP

ONEATA

CENTRAL DIVISION

YANUCA   BEQA

WESTERN DIVISION

VATULELE

KADAVU   PASSAGE

SOLO

DRAVUNI

BULIA

ONO

SOUTH

KADAVU

MATANUKU

MOALA

TOTOYA

MATUKU

PACIFIC

ONEATA   PASSAGE

OLORUA

TAVU-NA-SICI

VUAQAVA

KABARA

MARABO

FULAGA

MOCE

KOMO   KARONI

BOUNTY   BOAT   PASSAGE

NAMUKA-I-LAU

NAVUTU-I-RA   YAGASA LEVU

NAVUTU-I-LOMA

OGEA LEVU

OGEA DRIKI

OCEAN

INSET

| VATOA |
| ONO-I-LAU |
| TUVANA-I-COLO |
| TUVANA-I-RA |

NEW GUINEA   New Ireland   GILBERT Is   PHOENIX Is

Nauru I   SANTA CRUZ Is   ELLICE Is   TOKELAU Is

CORAL SEA   NEW HEBRIDES COND   Vanua Levu   FIJI Is   TONGA Is

QUEENSLAND   New Caledonia

AUSTRALIA   PACIFIC

NEW SOUTH WALES   Norfolk I

OCEAN   Kermadec Is

NEW ZEALAND

E180°W

NANUKU   PASSAGE

LAKEBA   PASSAGE

LANDS & SURVEY DIVISION
MINISTRY OF LANDS & MINERAL RESOURCES, FIJI

MRS. S. NA.